Feng Shui Made Easy

He ho ho
Merry Christmas
1995

♡ Sam

Feng Shui Made Easy

DESIGNING YOUR
LIFE WITH THE
ANCIENT ART OF
PLACEMENT

William Spear

HarperSanFrancisco
An Imprint of HarperCollins*Publishers*

HarperSanFrancisco and the author, in association with The Basic Foundation, a not-for-profit organization whose primary mission is reforestation, will facilitate the planting of two trees for every one tree used in the manufacture of this book.

A TREE CLAUSE BOOK

Illustrations copyright © 1995 by Sharon Rothman

FIRST EDITION
Library of Congress Cataloging-in-Publication Data:
Spear, William.
Feng shui made easy : designing your life with the ancient art of placement / William Spear.
p.   cm.
ISBN 0–06–251023–1 (pbk.)
1. Feng-shui.   2. I ching.   I. Title.
BF1779.F4S65   1995   133.3'33—dc20
                                                                95-17255

95   96   97   98   99   ❖   RRD/H   10   9   8   7   6   5   4   3   2   1

This book is dedicated to my father, with love,
and to the millions of men and women who have devoted
their lives to care for Mother Earth, with gratitude.

Contents

Acknowledgments

It is an honor to express here my deep appreciation and heartfelt thanks to the many people who have made this book possible. Gathering material for this book really began long before I realized that I would write it—preceding my focus on feng shui and the extraordinary body of knowledge that surrounds it. Like many young boys, I did not realize as a child how greatly my father's fascination with one particular subject would influence me later in life; now, as a grown man with sons of my own, I can still see the sparkle in his eyes that was present when we worked on magic squares together. It has had a lasting influence. This book is dedicated to him.

Many close friends, teachers, and colleagues have influenced me greatly, especially since the early 1970s, when I first went to Europe. Each has made a unique contribution to my understanding of life, philosophy, history, architecture, geomancy, design, and healing. Jens Bloch, in Copenhagen, taught me that life *is* magic; John Sunderland, an architect from Australia, inspired me with his own personal odyssey more than he ever knew. Countless friends too numerous to mention—all members of a very special Family—remain warmly in my memory as I recall the years I spent in Cincinnati, Ohio. To all of them, I offer my thanks.

Michio and Aveline Kushi stand alone as teachers whose lives and tireless efforts on behalf of so many people are of immeasurable value. I am most grateful for their support and friendship of over twenty-five years. Michael Rossoff and Jeanne Sloane opened their hearts and home to me, providing constant encouragement and support in my development. I offer my warmest thanks to both of them. Takashi Yoshikawa helped me to deepen my understanding in many ways and continues to be an invaluable source of wisdom. Carol Anthony, whom I have never even met, remains a mentor in the study of divination and meditation. Her writings on the *I Ching* are among the most clear and insightful available.

In my work as a teacher of feng shui and offering consultations to private clients, many groups and individuals have been very helpful. The staff and volunteers of the Community Health Foundation in London, the International Macrobiotic Institute in Switzerland, and the Australian School of Macrobiotics, especially Roger Green, the director, have been enormously generous in their support of my efforts. All of them, and the thousands of students who have attended my seminars, have been an inspiration to me. Malca Narol aided me greatly in organizing the outline of the original workbook for this manuscript, and Ron Rosenthal helped me to move through my early hesitations about the entire project. I thank them both for their support.

. Erica Smith at Harper Collins in London was instrumental in helping me simplify the subject; Lisa Bach at Harper San Francisco provided a genuine enthusiasm when she joined the project; Virginia Rich made editorial changes without which this book would have been unreadable; and Rosana Francescato was extremely helpful in organizing the final manuscript and inserting last-minute changes. Sharon Rothman cheerfully sketched many more illustrations than appear herein; they will grace my office walls as a constant reminder of the fun we had with case histories. Elaine Colvocoresses and Maryann O'Hara, my personal assistants in my office, both work consistently as extraordinary professionals and dedicated staff. I thank all of these individuals for their contributions on my behalf.

Gina Lazenby, my friend, colleague, and assistant in London, has been unconditional in her support and efforts to bring this unique subject the attention it deserves. I am very grateful for her dedication. My students in the Intuitive Feng Shui Professional Training Program throughout the world have challenged my every word, constantly calling me to task in their search for clarity. Each of them have given me far more than they may realize. I thank them all for their feedback and valuable comments. Closer to home and the heart, I thank my mother, Martha Ringel, for her encouragement and the corrections she made to the first manuscript. She would have made a great editor! My sister, Patricia Lemer, made invaluable suggestions following her review of my writings that resulted in a clarity of organization throughout the entire book. Her support was always available, for which I feel very blessed. The reader should be absolutely clear that the contributions of all of those whom I have mentioned, and the few I may have inadvertently omitted who helped me in writing this book, were exclusively in style, context, and order. Any inaccuracies, lack of clarity, or oversights are mine alone.

To my amazing family, I offer my deepest thanks and love. Jonah, Joshua, and Micah have seen me come and go at all hours of the day and night, while working, traveling, and writing. I was relieved when the book was completed, especially after Joshua asked me late one night between seminars in Europe and California if I was just visiting or home to stay. And to my wife, Joan, my everlasting love for all that she has given and continues to provide through her endless support, constant encouragement, and lifelong commitment.

William Spear
Litchfield, Connecticut
Spring 1995

Introduction

During World War II, my father was a cryptoanalyst who never left Washington, D.C., where he and his army buddies labored over codes intercepted from the enemy. Univac computers as big as a house were still no match for the human brain. He adored puzzles, games of Twenty Questions, crosswords, codes of any kind, and challenging mathematical problems.

Before I could count past ten, Dad showed me a way numbers could move in a special pattern. Sitting down with paper and pencil, he taught me how to construct a magic square. Tic-tac-toe got old fast, but with the "secret pattern," I could create magic squares all day.

Every number in every square had to be placed following the *pattern* of movement we learned from Dad. He taught my sister and me the spatial arrangement of the whole—how each part related to all the others. When we filled in the magic square, the pattern began to emerge—columns and rows were in relationship; beginnings and endings were not accidental. Everything fit because of the "rules." We could tell at a glance if something was "off."

When I was given coded messages, I had to consider the rules of *probability*. Common words like *I* or *the* were starting points, and a good understanding of sentence structure made breaking the codes much easier. We began passing notes in code; I was expected to respond using the code, which at first was not hard to break.

I had probability, integration, and visualization spoon-fed to me before I stepped into kindergarten. By playing with secret codes, we learned the statistical frequency of vowels and consonants in sentences, double-letter possibilities, sequences of words, and a myriad of other code-breaking tricks. A magical world—open only to those who knew the secret code—was beginning to form.

My sister and I would sit for hours assembling jigsaw puzzles on the coffee table. An early puzzle might be 50 pieces depicting a golden puppy on a pale green pillow; soon, there were 250- and 500-piece puzzles of flower gardens and jars of jellybeans—considerably more challenging. When we'd master these, before a new one was purchased, we'd turn all the pieces over and do it in green or gray using only shapes as our guide. We solved simple crosswords handily in our spare time; cryptograms and mazes from children's magazines we handled with ease. Soon, we tackled the more complex offerings from the local newspapers or the back pages of Sunday magazines. And our magic squares grew rapidly, soon covering hundreds of numbers at a time. We knew the pattern, the way, the secret. No doubt, Dad was completely unaware of the connection I would make years later.

At summer camp when I was fifteen, I came across a copy of the strangest book I'd ever seen. One of my camp counselors was reading—or more like talking to—a Chinese book of fortune-telling called the *I Ching*. Part of each chapter made absolutely no sense—things about farmers on their way to the market, the wagon wheel breaking, the sun beginning to rot the fruit, and so on. But the *explanations* that followed these parts were very intriguing.

"Sometimes, when we start to do something we really want, we run into difficulty at the beginning . . . our commitment is challenged, and we can lose it all . . . perseverance furthers . . ." Almost every chance I could—especially at night—I'd read a few lines from some chapter while the other kids in my cabin read comic books or had pillow fights. Some days, I'd even sneak away from a soccer game and return to the cabin to pull out my counselor's worn copy of the *I Ching* and read some more.

And then, one day, lightning struck. I turned to the introduction and saw it: the diagram of the philosophical foundation on which this oracle was based. This, it said, was the pattern of life itself, and the origin of the *Book of Change*. It was the magic square!

$$
\begin{array}{ccc}
4 & 9 & 2 \\
3 & 5 & 7 \\
8 & 1 & 6
\end{array}
$$

Nine numbers, arranged on the tic-tac-toe board I'd spent hours expanding, promised to contain the whole universe! It was a way of thinking and seeing so complete, so simple and harmonious, that a quarter of the world's population had used it to develop an entire cosmology, containing a unified theory of medicine, religion, economics, science, and art lasting thousands of years. *This* was the ultimate book of magic.

Soon, I got my own copy of the *I Ching* and learned how to use it. "Where one leg is short, the other is long," said the oracle, so it was not long before I began to see the two worlds of spirit and matter. I understood from this obscure passage that the materialism so highly developed in the West was balanced by great poverty and economic hardship in the East; moreover, the presence of so many religious teachings and systems so highly developed in the East was balanced by societies in the West that were essentially bereft of the deeper appreciation of the invisible world.

Nothing had a greater impact on Chinese-American cultural exchange than the visit of an American president, Richard Nixon, to the People's Republic of China in 1972. Interest in Asian culture in the West blossomed. James Reston, a Pulitzer Prize–winning journalist, received acupuncture for postoperative pain following the emergency removal of his appendix while in China. He was there with Henry Kissinger setting up the president's impending visit. Recounting his experience, Reston wrote, "The hospital is an intensely human and vibrant institution. . . . Like everything else in China these days, it is on its way toward some different combination of the very old and the very new." I recall envisioning a growing exchange of Western science and philosophy with ancient tradition.

Indeed, following the president's visit, scholars in both the arts and the sciences soon began to have access to previously hidden texts of spiritual classics. Translations of the *I Ching* and Lao Tsu's classic on Taoism, the *Tao Te Ching,* became easily available. And Joseph Needham's extraordinary study, *Science and Civilisation in China,* published in 1956 and comprising tens of thousands of pages in many volumes, was added to the reference section of my local library.

While poring over Needham's work one afternoon at the University of Cincinnati, I came across a section in volume 2 on how the ancient Chinese used certain tools derived from the *I Ching* to locate the most auspicious site for building. The sages believed that many factors needed to be considered when siting a house, wrote Needham, but that "the forms of hills and the directions of watercourses, being the outcome of the molding influences of winds and waters, were the most important." This art of geomancy was called *feng shui* (literally, winds and waters) and was still widely practiced in many parts of the Far East. Much of its focus was on understanding an invisible energy called *chi* that permeates all living things. "The force and nature of the invisible currents . . . had to be considered." And one of the tools used, a compass called a *luo pan,* contained references to the building blocks of the *I Ching* and their arrangement, a "map" called a *bagua.* This map, again, showed the pattern of the magic square!

I searched for more information, finding copies of a wide variety of works on geomancy and the Chinese concept of invisible energy. I came across references to books with titles like *The Golden Box of Geomancy, Terrestrial Conformations for Palaces and Houses, Kuan's Geomantic Indicator, The Yellow Emperor's House-Siting Manual, Mysterious Principles of the Universe,* and *Agreeable Geomantic Aphorisms.* Most works dated back to the third century B.C.

After leaving college in 1971, I lived in Europe, where I soon became a serious student of the Unifying Principle, the *I Ching,* and feng shui. Encountering a group of Asian teachers who had begun their studies in Tokyo with the Japanese philosopher Georges Ohsawa, my attention shifted to matters of diet and health, and I became a practitioner of a way of life called macrobiotics.

By the mid-1980s, I was already lecturing on Nine Star Ki, the remarkable system of astrology developed from the *I Ching* and first introduced to me a few years before by Michio Kushi. I designed the offices and educational center where I offered classes entirely on the principles of feng shui. Visitors always commented favorably when they arrived—it was truly a remarkable space, designed in an octagonal shape and containing elements of magic and harmony no one could ever quite describe in words.

I began to offer my design ideas, based on my studies and my intuitive understanding of feng shui and the Unifying Principle, to others setting up retail businesses, offices, homes, and apartments. A drawing board was soon visible in the corner of my office, and graph paper was evident everywhere. A series of courses I offered on the *I Ching* and Nine Star Ki was enormously well received, and I began to develop seminars in the United Kingdom, Europe, and Canada as well as expanding a series of seminars in the United States.

At the same holistic retreat center where I'd taught my seminars the year before, a course was offered by Professor Yun Lin, a feng shui practitioner of the Tantric Black Hat sect of Tibetan Buddhism.

I watched feng shui students in amazement as they completely abandoned their own sense of aesthetics and design in favor of the Eastern motifs expressed so frequently in Yun Lin's seminars. During consultations in New York or London, I came across a number of cases in which "cures" employed to correct design imbalances directly conflicted with the culture and surroundings of the occupants. Small tin wind chimes were hung in apartments decorated with modern Italian furniture; bamboo flutes, placed at forty-five-degree angles under heavy beams, contrasted with Chippendale tables. Artifacts from Chinatown, purchased for less than ten dollars, were hung on doors next to walls holding paintings by Dutch masters worth millions. Magic mirrors, red cloths, envelopes, and boxes were being carefully positioned under beds to attract money and improve health. No wonder people were confused, and put off, by what was available on feng shui in print!

Something was very strange about the way things were being interpreted. Students of Michio Kushi would often abandon their common sense and practice something quite different from what Kushi was actually advocating. Caught in their own dogma, students of macrobiotics—like the followers of feng shui in the seminars I'd observed—would soon get into trouble. It was clear to me that the principles behind both macrobiotics and feng shui were not culturally specific to the Far East. I had encountered many other teachings on geomancy, architectural design, medicine, and health from Asia, Africa, northern Europe, and South America that never referred to feng shui or macrobiotics but were exactly the same practices. Although these disciplines offered the same foundation principles originating in a holistic cosmology, they were simply unrecognized in the West.

I began to see clients who were well known in business, entertainment, or the arts. My exploration of Tibetan Buddhism revealed to me more about the origin of feng shui and its use in environments where people were dying. Following an intensive training course with the Elisabeth Kübler-Ross Center in Virginia, I expanded my practice further to include spiritual care for the dying. The world of "life force" or *chi* became a very real experience in my life as I watched many people pass from this world.

In the late 1980s, I began to expand my seminars to include a "big view" of life—the real definition of macrobiotics–and in it, the study of human beings and their environments, their houses and the spaces where they work and live. Despite having read about feng shui, most students who attended my seminars seemed to have no real understanding of how they could change their own environments and lives.

All kinds of people—florists, bankers, store owners, lawyers, consultants, real estate agents, actors, farmers, architects, and interior designers—began to seek my advice. Large projects, ranging from the redesign of the world headquarters of an international bank to a central plaza of a European capital, challenged my ability to go beyond tin wind chimes and bamboo flutes. What I offered, it seemed, was working, as new clients appeared in a steady stream.

As I continued to offer seminars over the next few years, one thing became very clear to me: these principles work. Hundreds of letters from students attested to the success they had gained by making changes they learned about at the weekend seminars. Stories of improving relationships, healthy children, and new jobs were common. More than just a few miracles showed up in the mailbox, and students taking the intermediate courses stood up in front of strangers to tell their own stories of transformation. People approached me at breaks and after lectures, whispering the most extraordinary tales of change in their lives following the course. Most asked when I'd write a book.

Feng Shui Made Easy was created after a lifetime of solving puzzles. Making the most complicated things more accessible and easily understood was inbred in me; transforming philosophies and concepts into practical methods had been fascinating to me since childhood.

This book will be like a feng shui consultant coming into your own home. But *Feng Shui Made Easy* tells you more than just how to re-arrange your furniture, it tells you how to change your life—and that is what feng shui is really all about. This is a remarkable system for self-development and a practical tool for improving business and relationships. All you need to do is practice—*the energy flows by itself.*

There is nothing new under the sun, and this information is no exception. I am simply trying to present it clearly and with some personal insights. I have "reorganized" this timeless message, like furniture in a room or articles on a desk, so that the reader can begin to grasp the whole rather than just the many parts. I employ the verb *to feng shui* in a lot of what I do these days. Used in this way, *feng shui* can mean "to harmonize, bring into balance, organize in a natural pattern," rather than carry with it the mystifying superstition imposed on it by those who cannot understand what they cannot measure and see. This book, in fact, "feng shuis" feng shui. This body of knowledge is not a tangent of mysticism extracted from an ancient culture's wisdom; it is the very heart of an understanding of life and integrates the vital system on which all of us must depend: our environment.

This book will introduce you to *intuitive* feng shui—a way that could quite accurately be called *vital design*. It looks broadly at patterns over which we have absolutely no control, like the design of our solar system, and deeply into our own microcosm, down to the molecules of DNA. It is linked by the Unifying Principle, the unspoken backbone of ancient culture and religion. Most books about design and placement teach the reader *what*. This book is intended to add *how* and *why* and, in doing so, add a bit of magic to your life. Enjoy!

Chapter 1

A New Way of Being

Empty vessels make the most noise.
SIXTEENTH-CENTURY PROVERB

How to Read This Book

You have in your hand an instruction manual for creating and designing *living spaces*. Understanding one of the most important concepts of feng shui depends most of all on your ability to pretend (if necessary) that you know nothing and to observe your room and workplace from *emptiness*. Achieving this state of objectivity need not be difficult; we have all had moments when the slate was clean and we were open to any possibility. Recovering this perspective in order to look at our own home or office requires a bit of practice; for some it may be easy, for others, a real challenge.

If you keep doing what you've done before (in the past), you will keep getting (in the future) what you've always gotten. Something has to change, and with feng shui you have the opportunity to begin to relate to the outer world as if it were simply a reflection of the inner psyche. Symbols appear everywhere in our environment; indeed, to the trained eye, your space reveals much more about who you are than you might like! Physiognomy, or face-reading, and handwriting analysis are similar disciplines used to diagnose personality, but our faces and our handwriting are extremely difficult for us to change. Moving the position of a desk or changing the color of a wall is much easier and has far-reaching consequences, whether we are aware of them or not.

Feng shui is too powerful to ignore and too important to trivialize. In order to get the most from this book, read and study as much of the early chapters and exercises as you can *before* making any changes. Explore the invisible world in chapter 2. Reflect on the power of feng shui and its potential in your life in chapter 3. Establish your priorities as you are guided in chapter 4. Become familiar with the *I Ching* in chapter 5—it's easier than you think! Invite some friends over, and fill in the First Impressions Worksheet in chapter 6. Make sure you accurately place the key to feng shui, called the *bagua*, as detailed in chapter 7. Look at your own house again, using the guidelines in chapter 8. Look at your life again through the eyes of feng shui in chapter 9. Then what you do will be grounded in understanding. What happens when you place a cure will result from what *you* create.

Getting Started

If you are interested in the ordinary, then shopping in a store with decorators on staff may suit your needs. You may need to have them develop a particular style for you or pick the fabrics that, from their viewpoint, match other elements in your space. Perhaps you are concerned with being "in vogue," like the couple who worried that the renovation of their home would not be completed before the bleached white flooring they had chosen went out of style. Or maybe you are the design equivalent of being "tone deaf" in music and have no eye or taste that you can trust to be pleasant—let alone appropriate—without the guidance of a professional or an experienced friend. Recognizing the vast range of possibilities, you may be overwhelmed with information on design and balance and not feel well enough informed to practice feng shui without making a "mistake."

To get started, you may need to go backward. Clearing clutter and simplifying your life can make a huge difference. Washing those dusty slipcovers or throwing out that box of old belts and shoes in the front hall closet is what we all must do before the magic can take hold. Plan to get a little dirty at first and work up a sweat. Spring cleaning has just begun—regardless of the season!

Find a clear and orderly space to sit and read further, and make yourself comfortable. The longest of journeys begins with a single step.

Transformation

The world is ruled by letting things take their
course. It cannot be ruled by interfering.
LAO TSU, *Tao Te Ching*

Who you need to be to practice this remarkable philosophy is simply someone who recognizes *possibility*. Anything can happen, and you are not limited by your design experience, taste, belief system, bank account, or expectations. Energy flows by itself; changes occur on their own. Miracles happen. In effect, what you will learn to do is to get out of your own way. We are always in the process of creating our future life and destiny—nothing is already decided. Feng shui embraces free will and allows *you* to write the next chapter of your life. Some people, perhaps less pragmatic, refer to possibility as "dream." In that sense, logic defers to instinct, and the true measure of our success is likely to be anywhere but the bottom line.

How you need to be is open. Possibility does not exist unless you are willing to consider it. When someone says "I love you," you must have a response other than, "That's impossible!" It requires no belief to begin to live this way—just the smallest opening or space in which possibility can develop. Many times, people who begin to practice feng shui do not believe what happens, and that's fine. A new relationship or job comes along, shortly after they make some changes, and they tell their friends, "I can't believe this is happening! I bet this would have happened even if I *hadn't* made those changes!" It is not really a question of believing anything.

Georges Ohsawa, the Japanese philosopher who introduced macrobiotics to the West, taught a spirit of "noncredo"—one that is helpful to nurture. He felt that anything can happen (and does) according to basic laws in the universe that have more to do with the world of invisible spirit than the material world. When something does occur, you will *know* it, even if you still don't believe it, and you will begin to recognize the difference.

Setting Goals

Self-understanding is one of the main purposes of
philosophy—to understand the relationships of men,
things and words to each other.
ISAIAH BERLIN, *Conversations with Isaiah Berlin*

What do you want to change? Some who use this book will want to improve their life, income, and relationships; others may need a total makeover following a separation or loss, years of difficulty, and a long stream of "bad luck." Setting some goals at the beginning of this practice will help you to gain a perspective of your life now, as well as evaluate the inevitable changes that occur later.

GOAL-SETTING EXERCISE

Turn a blank sheet of paper sideways so that it is like a landscape spread out in front of you. Imagine that it is divided into four equal quadrants.

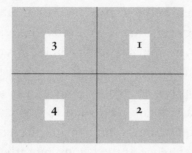

In the upper-right quadrant (one), write four words or phrases that best characterize your *current situation*. They can be positive or negative—"unemployed, angry at Mom, broke, stuck in a rut" or "reflective, busy all the time, feeling blessed, happily married." Any combination of positive, negative, or neutral words or phrases is fine. Be succinct and clear—don't take up the whole space.

Next, in the lower-right quadrant (two) write three or four positive words or phrases as goals you would like to achieve in three months. Put them down as statements: "I will get a new job," or "My Mom and I will resolve our differences and support each other," or "My income will increase from new business contacts." *Make up your own goals!* Avoid goals like "I will win the lottery," or "I will marry a billionaire heiress." (Wait until you are sure you'd really want to.) Be reasonable!

Finally, write down three long-term goals (one year) in the upper-left quadrant (three). These could be much more lofty, like "I will embark on a whole new career path," or "I will marry the man of my dreams." Take a chance, and be a bit *un*reasonable! In quadrant four, write the words "The past is over."

Putting Feng Shui in Your Life

More than just the practice of geomancy, placement, or spatial arrangement, feng shui is also a philosophy or a way of seeing the world. It is important at the start to be both inquisitive and flexible, asking how things fit together as you move toward an ability to see the whole; however, as understanding comes, it is essential *not* to put your life in feng shui. Doing so almost always results in the creation of a mechanical monster, one that sees life as a series of fixed pictures and set patterns—a sure and fast road to arrogance. As extraordinary as this philosophy may seem to you, put feng shui in your life only as a point of reference at the beginning rather than the sole operating system.

For example, an architect or designer can use feng shui *after* he or she has used the creativity and skill needed to do the job. Then, as if putting on a new pair of 3-D glasses, the creator can look at the drawings using feng shui as a guideline and see what changes might need to be made. Do not try to create the ideal using feng shui as the template, as it will surely limit the creativity you need to come up with a unique design.

So much of what has come to us from ancient cultures has become dogmatic and, as such, limiting. When used appropriately, feng shui provides us with unlimited possibility in life, constantly changing and flowing, never restricting, always guiding. Beware of a tendency at first to "know" more than you have experienced. Observe, reflect, and build on your personal involvement with your surroundings and their relation to your life. You will soon see that no one could possibly know your own truth better than you. Feng shui will become, like a trusted old friend, an invaluable resource of wisdom and inspiration that simply gives you a new way of seeing your life.

The worksheet on the next page can be used as a prelude to making design changes in your home or office. After completing the worksheet, you will have a clearer idea of which areas of your life you might change using feng shui.

SELF-EVALUATION WORKSHEET

In each of the nine sections, read the description, then, in the four groups of phrases below it, find the one that comes closest to speaking your truth. Every phrase need not be exactly like one you might use. To keep track of your answers, circle a letter—A, B, C, or D— for each area on the Answer Form that follows the worksheet.

1. How do you feel about the work you are doing? Is your job in the field you want it to be in? Are you fulfilled by your work and acknowledged by the people around you in relation to your work? Are you considering a career change? These questions all relate to the area of your life that feng shui calls *Water*.

THE JOURNEY

Water has to do with your path, your journey, the flow, or *tao,* of your life, as if you are in a boat, sailing along through the years. It is not just your present job: you may be an aspiring artist working as a clerk temporarily while you wait for your first big break. And it does not relate to your salary or paycheck as a measure of success. This question evaluates your place on the "river of life"—whether you feel safe in the boat, whether you are flowing with or against the tide, crashing into or gliding by the rocks.

A. Life flows along quite well. I'm on the right road. I'm doing the work I want to do, I feel acknowledged by my coworkers. I am satisfied with the work I do. I feel productive. I have a good job. I feel fortunate to be doing what I really want to do and enjoying it. I feel I'm sailing on a beautiful ocean liner!

B. As above, but less so.

C. As below, but less so.

D. I feel like a salmon swimming upstream—definitely against the flow. I do not have a job. I am working, but not doing what I want. I'm thinking about going into a whole new field. My résumé is out there, but I am not getting any calls. I don't like my job and am looking for a new one. I haven't had much luck in the workplace these days. Help! I'm drowning!

RELATIONSHIP

2. How are your relationships with your friends, spouse, and colleagues? Are you single with an active social life, or are you isolated, finding it difficult to meet anyone? How is your marriage? Is it a fulfilling partnership? Are you considering separation? Recently divorced? Blissfully in love? Desperately seeking? These questions relate to the area of your life called *Earth*.

The meaning of this area is receptivity, the ideal state in which relationships develop. It has to do with all partnerships, close associations both platonic and professional, and marriage, though not just matrimony as such. This question looks at relationships in general, whether they are going along well or with great difficulty, whether there are a number of eligible choices or none.

A. My relationships are great. I get a lot of attention from my mate. My social life is very active. My spouse is wonderful. I meet new people every week who ask me out. I feel as if we are still on our honeymoon. The phone hardly ever stops ringing. I'm recently engaged.

B. As above, but less so.

C. As below, but less so.

D. My social life is a disaster. I've tried everything to meet my match, but there just doesn't seem to be anyone interested. I feel jinxed. I'm in the process of separating. I just moved to town and have found it very difficult to meet new people—one date is easy, but they never call back. I thought celibacy would be more fun than this. I'm thinking about taking vows!

ELDERS

3. How would you characterize your relationship with your parents? Do you have a meaningful relationship with a teacher, mentor, or elder whom you consider an important part of your life? Even if one or both of your parents are deceased, how do you carry the memory of your life with them in your mind today? This area of life is represented by the symbol for *Thunder*. Like the resonating bass of thunder that comes before a rainstorm, this question also relates to

the foundation or root that preceded you, the ancestors who came before you and, in particular, your mother and father. It corresponds to our concern for family, parents, elders, teachers, and those in a superior position, such as your supervisor.

A. I get along very well with both my parents. I had a special relationship with one of my grandparents. My boss at work is a great supervisor. I have a mentor from college with whom I still keep in touch. I have a lot of teachers I highly respect. My dad died a while back; we finally came to peace over a lot of unresolved issues before he passed on. I'm grateful for so much my parents gave me. I have a deep respect for my ancestors.

B. As above, but less so.

C. As below, but less so.

D. I haven't spoken to my parents in years. My grandfather was a horrible man, and I never liked him. My boss is mean and insensitive. My mom and I argue all the time. My teachers never liked me. I don't usually get along very well with old people. One or both of my parents never really loved me very much. Don't ask!

4. How often in your life do you feel blessed? Is money a real problem for you, or are you not terribly concerned with your bank account? Do you have positive cash flow, or are you always in debt? Do you feel fortunate, or are you on a seemingly endless streak of bad luck? This area of life feng shui calls *Wind*. It generates the energy of blessings from the material world—not just in hard cash but in the general sense of fortune or "good omens" creating a state of auspiciousness. The wind brings good luck in the form of fortunate blessings from the material world.

FORTUNATE
BLESSINGS

A. I feel blessed with good fortune nearly every day. I make money and have a good income. People call me lucky. Money is really not a problem for me. Things show up just when I need them.

B. As above, but less so.

C. As below, but less so.

D. I'm broke. I could barely pay my rent last month. I do not have a job. I'm pretty far in debt right now. When it comes to luck, I'm having a bad streak these days. It's really hard to pay the bills recently. Blessed? Ha! How 'bout cursed!

UNITY

5. The central number 5, falling in the middle of the cardinal numbers 1 through 9, relates to the area of life called the *Tai Chi*. Regarded as the center of the universe, the Tai Chi is the place where heaven and earth meet and divide, creating the very breath of life force and all the other elements. There is no direct way to evaluate this area other than as a sum of the parts, because the Tai Chi has a part of every one of the eight other energies in it. A special section in chapter 9 talks in greater detail about the significance of this central area.

HELPFUL
FRIENDS

6. Do you have a lot of close friends or helpers you can depend on in a crisis? Do you consider yourself helpful to others? Are you generous and supportive with your time and money, serving either as a volunteer, donor, or patron to a group less fortunate? Are there lots of people in your life who show up as helpful friends or "angels" of the visible and invisible type? This area of our life is symbolized by the word *Heaven* and relates in the broadest sense to philanthropy.

Like a gift from heaven, the selfless acts of volunteers, friends, and "angels" in our lives are beyond measure; at the same time, our efforts as helpful friends in the unconditional service of others is truly one of life's greatest blessings.

A. I am an active volunteer in many organizations, giving both my time and money whenever I can. Many friends would do anything for me, as I would for them. Sometimes I feel I have a guardian angel watching over me. I try to give generously to those in need. A lot of people have helped me in times of trouble. I am amazed that, whatever you give, you always receive much more in return.

B. As above, but less so.

C. As below, but less so.

D. When I'm down and out, I'm on my own. I'd like to help others more, sure, but I'm just so busy and I barely get by myself. People don't usually think of me as someone to depend on for support. I don't have many free hands who volunteer their time to help our group. Everyone is in it for the money. Giving unconditionally is impossible. UFOs are all a government plot. There no such thing as an angel except in fairy tales.

7. Are you creative? Do you have children? How are your various projects going? Do you have "writer's block," or do the ideas seem to pour out onto the paper? As a parent, is your relationship with your offspring rich and joyful, or full of turmoil and sadness? This area of life corresponds to the image of the *Lake*.

CREATIVITY

Here, the energy of creativity gathers, making possible the children, ideas, and projects to which we give birth and all that springs forth from the deepest internal spring that feeds our life. The joy and beauty we see in all that we create are characterized by this open energy, carrying also, like our children, a great depth of spirit.

A. My children are everything to me. I am very creative. I have no shortage of ideas or projects. Kids are great, and even though I don't have any, I really love them. As an artist, my creativity is my life, and I am very fortunate to be blessed with lots of it.

B. As above, but less so.

C. As below, but less so.

D. Children should be seen, but not heard. I haven't had a new idea in years. We're having trouble conceiving. I can write poems, but I usually feel pretty blocked. The last big project I worked on failed miserably. I want kids, but I think I'm infertile. My children and I don't get along at all. I feel less creative than a block of wood.

CONTEMPLATION

8. What is your relationship with the spiritual world? Do you meditate, pray, or chant regularly? Are you an atheist, an agnostic, or a devout skeptic? Are you an active member of your church or temple, attending regular services and observing religious holidays? Our capacity for inner stillness is called the *Mountain* and signifies meditation, contemplation, and introspection.

It is not necessarily about organized religion or beliefs but relates more to our sense of the sacred and spiritual in life, often felt most strongly in the solitude of a mountain or cave where we can tune into ourselves.

A. My life is full of spiritual meaning. I meditate every day. I love reading scripture and teachings of the masters. I am religious in my own way. I've done a lot of searching in this area, through many avenues, and have gone through lots of changes. Life is a mystery.

B. As above, but less so.

C. As below, but less so.

D. I'm pretty skeptical about what science can't prove. I'd like to meditate, but I'm too busy. Books on religion and the "spiritual" world bore me. I used to believe in God, but now I'm not so sure. What you see is all there is; the rest is all manufactured for mass consumption. The New Age is a marketing ploy. Prayer makes no difference in my life. God is dead. I don't understand this part.

ILLUMINATION

9. Do you care what other people think of you? Are you recognized in your field for the work you do? Are you fulfilled in life, or is there something still missing? Do you feel that all the answers to your problems are inside you, or do you need the guidance of others who "know" more? If you learned that you might die very soon, how do you suppose your life would change? The final area concerns the energy of *Fire* and relates to illumination or enlightenment.

Sometimes referred to—inadequately—as Fame, this area is more than just reputation or prominence; it has to do with the light that shines within. As the time comes when our lives draw to a close, we will understand more fully the meaning of enlightenment, as we grow closer to an inner brightness often present in the eyes of an elder sage. So, although the spotlight of media attention makes a movie star or a politician famous, being in the light is more about illumination within than public recognition.

A. Every day is another miracle. Sometimes life feels like a dream. I have a good sense of myself and do not live to please others. I am usually very clear about my direction in life. People find me a source of inspiration. I feel contented to be alone, even though I enjoy other people in my life, too. My good intuition is a sign of my clarity.

B. As above, but less so.

C. As below, but less so.

D. How others feel about me matters a lot. I feel confused about half the time. Someone will show me how. Nobody really respects me for the work I do. It will be a long time before I'm anywhere near enlightenment. Death is a terrifying concept to me, and I am not ready, no way, not yet, please. Yeah, sure, me and the Dalai Lama are good buddies—*not!*

Circle your answers on this form before moving on to the next section.

Water	1.	A B C D
Earth	2.	A B C D
Thunder	3.	A B C D
Wind	4.	A B C D
Tai Chi	5.	No response necessary
Heaven	6.	A B C D
Lake	7.	A B C D
Mountain	8.	A B C D
Fire	9.	A B C D

Putting Your Priorities into Perspective

Once you have completed the Self-Evaluation Worksheet, it should be easier to see the areas in your life that are the most important to approach with feng shui. If, for example, you circled *D* under Thunder and *C* under Lake and *A* or *B* for the other areas, then these are the priorities that will need to be addressed in your living environment. The space around us is a reflection of our inner world, so it is very likely that when you identify the actual areas of your house ruled by the energies of Thunder and Lake, you will see ways to change and improve this part of your living (and working) space.

Exactly what to do with this information will depend upon your ability to begin to relate to the invisible world of energy around you in much the same way you have explored the vibrational and emotional world within. An additional worksheet in chapter 4 will guide you in doing just that.

Chapter 2

A Language for the Invisible World

Look, it cannot be seen—it is beyond form.
Listen, it cannot be heard—it is beyond sound.
Grasp, it cannot be held—it is intangible.
These three are indefinable;
Therefore they are joined in one.

LAO TSU, Tao Te Ching

What Is Feng Shui?

As modern society begins to discover traditional medicine, scientists and medical researchers continue to broaden their focus by considering the effect of the environment on individual health and well-being. The entire field of design and house building has already been radically changed by studies showing that potentially toxic elements are used in many common building materials. Background radiation emitted by high-tension wires, radar guns, or other sources, documented as a contributing cause of some cancers, is now a serious concern. Investigations into the effects of color and light on human behavior have helped many interior designers create more harmonious environments for home and workplace.

The integration of the outside world and our internal environment is a cornerstone of most traditional philosophies. The Japanese saying *Shin do fu ji* (literally, soil and man not two) reminds us of the unity of human beings and the earth. Indigenous people all over the globe have always understood that we are not separate from our planet, our homes, or one another. Through in-depth study of the principles of unity and observation of the timeless perfect order in the universe, feng shui brings together the external and internal environments by creating balanced, peaceful dwellings whose occupants can develop health and happiness.

In Asia in the earliest times, masters of the art of placement were originally employed to locate the most auspicious site for the tomb of a departed loved one. After the general area was selected by the family, the feng shui master would arrive with a *luo pan,* or diviner's compass, and locate a site perfectly situated between mountain ranges, near the bend of a river, or in a valley where the ancestral spirits could be in harmony with heaven and earth. A tomb would be built there and blessed, and the family's good fortune would be enhanced by the effect on future generations of the properly cared-for spirit.

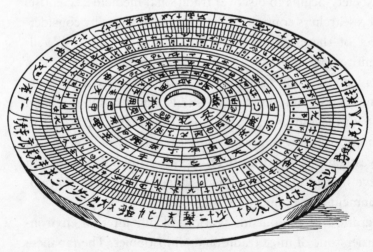

LUO PAN COMPASS

Over time, this classical practice of feng shui grew to include detailed observation of the living world and the way in which earth's energy affects all of daily life. Good feng shui meant prosperity and long life—a conscious connection between the outside environment and the world within. Considered part of the philosophy of the *I Ching,* feng shui remained an integral part of daily life until Western influences and political change began to erode this long-held, deep appreciation for the invisible.

The World of Vibrations

The gentle wind does move, silently, invisibly.
WILLIAM BLAKE

All matter has vibration. Referred to as *chi* by the Chinese, *ki* by the Japanese, and *prana* or *brahmin* by the peoples of India, this invisible electromagnetic energy radiates in particular patterns from objects of all shapes and sizes. Detailed maps of chi in the body reveal pathways of energy called meridians and form the basis of the practice of acupuncture and shiatsu massage therapy.

In the experience of an amputee known as phantom pain, a knee itches that is not there to itch. Even though the whole leg has been removed, the energy that created it still remains. This phenomenon can be demonstrated through the use of Kirlian photography. A picture of a leaf using a Kirlian camera shows the "energy" of the leaf radiating from its edges. Cut off a corner of the leaf, and a new picture will still show the whole leaf, even though a part is now missing in the material plane.

This invisible energy, this vibration, flows constantly through all life forms. It has been closely observed and carefully detailed in the seven energy chakras observed in Ayurvedic medicine and the acupuncture meridians detailed in traditional Chinese medicine—

both for thousands of years. Our earth has similar meridians, called ley lines, and concentrated power points that even in relatively recent times were acknowledged as places of great energy and spirit where great cathedrals and shrines were erected by our ancestors. A day in Avebury, a small village in Great Britain where early inhabitants erected huge stone monoliths reflecting the movements of the sun and moon in relation to the earth, should convince most skeptics of the significance of this energy. It is a site of incredible power, where this energy is intensely focused; indeed, all over the globe these sites are now being explored and appreciated for their potential healing qualities. Although recognized long ago, these qualities are now all but forgotten, with so much attention being paid to technology and material gain.

Divination

The geomancer's compass, the divining tool employed by the classical master, displayed the eternal pattern of the spiral, which reflected the infinite movement of chi between heaven and earth.

After positioning the eight or more rings to align with the directions, rivers, or mountain ranges, the feng shui master could detect blockages or surges of chi much as a dowser does using a divining rod or an acupuncturist using pulse diagnosis. The geomancer would then make suggestions for the shape or orientation of a dwelling and the placement of entrance ways and other design features, such as the location of bedrooms or kitchens, for the most harmonious environment. An astrological analysis of the occupants was studied because many decisions would always depend upon the inhabitants' occupations, the proposed use of the rooms, and the overall understanding of the more subtle aspects of the invisible world.

Intuitive Feng Shui

Although the art of placement is still widely practiced in some parts of Asia, the classical school employing the geomancer's compass is less evident in the West. In its place, *intuitive* feng shui is fast becoming popular among designers, architects, and many in the healing arts who acknowledge the relationship between environment and health. Rooted in a universal cosmology like Eastern philosophy, intuitive feng shui can help you learn how to practice "acupuncture in space." The success of this practice depends upon the clarity and understanding of the designer—you—based on your experience rather than your knowledge. Where there are blockages, practitioners can open pathways for energy flow by making various adjustments—just as in acupuncture. In order to activate or sedate energy, the practitioner carefully scrutinizes colors, shapes, textures, patterns, and materials, much as your diet would be reviewed as a factor affecting your *internal* environment.

This practice also relies on an understanding of the arrangement of space detailed in the *I Ching*. If it is used as a point of reference in the design process, architects using feng shui can create extraordinarily powerful structures setting the stage for the occupant's good fortune. Many constantly imitated modern architects remain on the cutting edge due, in part, to the great advantage this profound wisdom brings. However, a building that looks similar to one created using feng shui principles but is designed without an understanding of the whole can easily create a nightmare for its occupants.

Intuitive feng shui is distinguished from the classical approach by the practitioner's focus on instinct, feeling, and intuition. These three forces, constantly at work in every individual, are the precise source of the inherent wisdom that created the cosmological philosophies of all ancient cultures. Rather than trying to analyze and interpret complex systems of energy or culturally specific directives from another time and place, the practitioner of intuitive feng shui learns to uncover the ever-present wisdom *within*. Changes are made based on clarity, judgment, and the elusive storehouse of intuition to which we all have direct access. Interestingly, the Japanese characters for the word *intuition* mean, literally, "original ability."

Chapter 3

Places of Power

*A direct and superficial examination of things does
not always enable us to conclude that reality is
identical with perception.*
LECOMTE DU NOÜY, Human Destiny

A Bit of History

Some of the most extraordinary monuments of ancient life on earth
can be found among the rolling hills of Great Britain just a few
hours' drive from London. For those who have visited these unusual
sites, Stonehenge, Avebury, and Silbury Mound are not easily forgotten—even though their significance may not have been fully understood. Scholars the world over have devoted thousands of hours of
research and study to setting forth various theories of why these sites
were constructed and what they might have meant to the inhabitants
of our planet who designed and erected them.

It is agreed, however, that these landmarks are among dozens
more in this region that fall along a perfectly straight line that one
can easily see by examining a map of the area. No doubt the ancients
were able to discern a concentration of some type of energy that ran
through the region. That they erected monoliths, earthen mounds,

temples, and church naves *precisely* on this line can hardly be written off as mere coincidence. Just what they were up to—the *why* of it all—is still in question.

The Forces of Heaven and Earth

Energy, or chi, is an effect of the force from either heaven or earth. It is always moving in the pattern of a spiral, and we can easily visualize it by observing phenomena on the planet from the point of view of astronauts in outer space. From amid the spiral of our own solar system, a look down at the planet Earth reveals swirling cloud patterns, the funnel clouds of hurricanes and tornadoes, and the movement of oceans. In the northern hemisphere, this spiral moves counterclockwise; that is, water will go down the drain in the direction opposite to that of the movement of a clock. Cross the equator, however, and the movement changes to clockwise—still spiraling, but in the opposite direction to movement above the equator.

As we look more closely at life on Earth, we can see nature's expression of this pattern everywhere: the antlers of an elk, the design of the branches of a tree, a seashell's form, the structure of creation itself. In human beings, this emerging pattern begins with the movement of sperm and egg—in a spiral—and is imprinted in our bodies hundreds of times. Fingerprints, hair growth, esophageal lining, nerve fibers, sexual organs, cardiac tissue—it is in everything, down to the double helix of our most basic building blocks, the spiral of DNA.

This irrefutable pattern of the universe, manifesting from space (heaven's force) and from the earth itself (earth's force) is the expression of chi energy harnessed in prehistoric times with the building of monuments like Stonehenge and Silbury Mound. Modern technology now permits us to measure the intensity of this energy, validating—for skeptics, at least—the existence of something unusual on these sites.

Like Avebury nearby, Silbury Mound was placed by human beings to concentrate *earth's force* and in so doing attract more of heaven's force to the site. The monoliths placed in a particular pattern at Stonehenge and Avebury are magnets to *heaven's force,* an act of acknowledging life itself. Here, no doubt, were festivals, celebrations, birthing rituals, observances of summer solstices and autumnal equinoxes enhanced by the proper placement of objects to intensify this vibrational field.

In contrast to this attracting of the living force of heaven, sites near Avebury and other sites on the Stonehenge Ley were used for quite a different purpose. One example, called the Longbarrows, is a long, cavelike tunnel, equally mysterious to most modern city folk, who try to understand what *is* there rather than what *is not* there.

The Longbarrows has quite a different energy present: it was designed and constructed to harness earth's force as it rises upward in the invisible world of chi. Inside the cave tunnel, small cubicles lead to a central "altar" where the ancients could take advantage of the intense concentration of the same force present when a human being's time on earth ends. Here, and in similarly charged locations throughout the world, our ancestors would sit to meditate, becoming one with the essence of their true nature and gracefully detaching from their physical form.

As we die, our final breath is inward and upward. These early astral travelers might have practiced in the outer cubicles and, when their time came to depart for the next world, taken their position at the altar and "blasted off" with the concentration of earth's force focused beneath them.

Not a cemetery, burial ground, or tomb of any sort, the Longbarrows was simply a place where life on Earth would end and the physical form would be discarded. Even the Romans, at the foundation of their cities, constructed a vertical shaft with a rounded roof, not unlike Longbarrows, where the departed spirits might receive gifts from the living, ensuring a continuity of generations.

Making Conscious Choices

Though we may not be interested in creating an environment in our home or office that makes it possible to leave our body for astral travel, or to capture an energy appropriate for celebration of life, it is clear that such distinctly different activities can be enhanced through a careful understanding of the elements present in the environment to focus the force of heaven or earth. In fact, some bedrooms where occupants complain of insomnia have too much heaven's force—not because they are sited over a ley line or on top of a man-made mound, but because of the choice of colors, shapes, textures, patterns, and placement in the overall design. And some offices where workers commonly complain of fatigue are environments that feel more like a barrows—the result of architectural and interior design choices that were made unconsciously yet that powerfully affect human behavior.

The practice of feng shui enables you to create environments suitable for their intended activity. It empowers you to correct already

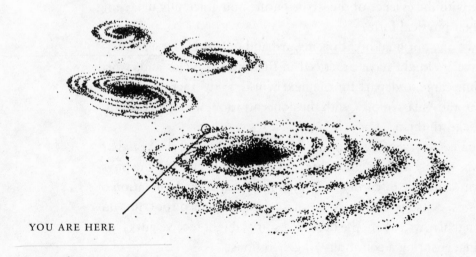

YOU ARE HERE

existing imbalances in order to improve your life. The understanding necessary to achieve these results, however, requires looking at the world in a completely different way—largely misunderstood in Western culture—that focuses as much on what is *not* there as on what *is* there. Many people are so sure of their reality—so locked into seeing the world a certain way—that it is extremely difficult for them to leave behind a way of seeing the world that fits "the norm."

The Story of the Well Frog

Once upon a time, there was a frog who lived in a well behind a small house in the woods. One day, when the frog was hopping around his home, he came upon another frog, whom he had never seen before.

"Who are you—and where did you come from?" he asked the other frog.

"I am from the ocean," the new frog replied.

"The ocean? What is that like?" asked the Well Frog.

"It's big," said the Ocean Frog.

"Big! How big? Is it as big as, say, a quarter of my well?"

"It is," the Ocean Frog quickly responded, adding "even bigger. . . ."

"Well, then! Is it as big as half my well?" asked the Well Frog, now with more confidence.

"Yes, my friend, it is even bigger than half!"

"Bigger still? Incredible! Can you show me this place where you live, this ocean you call home?"

"Of course," said the Ocean Frog, "but you'll have to leave the well and follow me!"

"OK, let's go there!" said the Well Frog and hopped up the stones on the side of the well to join his new friend.

The Ocean Frog led the way to the very top of the well, jumped off the edge into the dirt, and headed off through the woods. The Well Frog followed close behind. At the edge of woods, they came to a clearing, and the Ocean Frog, not hesitating, hopped through the open field and over another hill, until he came to a sandy beach. There, at the edge of the water, the Ocean Frog turned around as the Well Frog arrived. They sat and looked out over the ocean.

"See," said the Ocean Frog, "this is the ocean where I live."

Whereupon the Well Frog looked out into the vast expanse that lay in front of him and exploded.

Once we leave home (what we know) and go beyond the limiting factors (walls, borders, or boundaries), anything can happen! When you begin to perceive the power of the invisible world, you may very well explode, too—with possibilities for a new future!

Feng Shui in Today's Environment

What we don't know about life covers a lot more territory than what we do know. The world of architecture and building design has changed dramatically over the past twenty years, due in part to the explosion of technology, computer-aided design, and major advances in understanding the importance of energy conservation. We have only just begun to sense the consequences of all of this, identifying some buildings as sick, some environments as plastic or artificial, and some materials as toxic. The tip of the iceberg—or edge of the ocean, if you will—has finally been reached as we enter an age when we are more aware of the impact of the energy we can't so easily measure.

Design that respects life and incorporates nature is a lot more than just a shopping mall with ramps for wheelchairs and lots of plants. Living design feels the way homemade bread smells: warm, delicious, and irresistible. Designers of the future may not turn their backs on computers but will, of necessity, use intuition, instinct, and creativity much more in order to build vital environments sensitive to the people who inhabit them. The understanding of energy flow, the forces of heaven and earth, sound waves, light, living objects, and even health will become far more important to our happiness and very existence than fad, fashion, or facades. What underlies every space is the living energy all of us feel. This is "feng shui" today—not just "wind and water" from an ancient culture a thousand years ago but the creation of living spaces like clear, fresh air and free-flowing water. Reuniting with the majesty and timeless presence of the energy of planet Earth, feng shui provides a means to harmonize opposites: heaven and earth, man and woman, instinct and intellect, outer and inner, being and the Divine.

Chapter 4

Is There a Doctor in the House?

There was a crooked man, and he walked a crooked mile,
He found a crooked sixpence against a crooked stile:
He bought a crooked cat, which caught a crooked mouse,
And they all lived together in a little crooked house.

J. O. HALLIWELL, 1842

Diagnosis

Living in a crooked house will make your life full of crooked things. Because who you are, the way you perceive your life, and what's going on now will be revealed in your environment, the Self-Evaluation Worksheet can be assessed in different ways. In order to have some indication of where to look in your house, the first step in *intuitive* feng shui is to ask questions about your life. If you scored all *A*'s, then there is really no need at this time to get an *A*+. But because each part of the whole is related in some way to every other part, like paired organs in the body or the complementary, antagonistic relationships that appear throughout the natural world, correcting just one thing will affect everything else in your life. A warm relationship with our parents greatly improves our chances of finding happiness with a significant other; doing what we want to do in life positively affects our sense of the invisible world of spirit. Don't be concerned if your score contains a few letters other than *A*—or no *A*'s at all!

Your Priorities List

The next step is to turn your Answer Form into a priorities list by writing down the numbers in descending order of score, leaving all *A*'s off your list. Suppose the Answer Form for your self-evaluation looks like the example that follows.

SELF-EVALUATION ANSWER FORM

Water	1. (A) B C D
Earth	2. A B C (D)
Thunder	3. A B C (D)
Wind	4. A B (C) D
Tai Chi	5. No response necessary
Heaven	6. A (B) C D
Lake	7. (A) B C D
Mountain	8. (A) B C D
Fire	9. A (B) C D

Your priorities list would then be 2, 3, 4, 6, 9—Earth, Thunder, Wind, Heaven, and Fire.

On the positive side, this would indicate that you are doing what you want to do, are on the right road, have a great job or are satisfied with the "journey" and gave yourself an *A* in Water. You also have a good relationship with your children, or feel very creative, or are not concerned with "offspring" and scored yourself an *A* in Lake, too. And with matters of spirit, you also feel good—perhaps you meditate, or attend church regularly, or have a healthy perception of spiritual things that caused you to grade the area known as Mountain with an *A*.

When the questions about relationship were evaluated, however, you gave yourself a *D* in Earth—either because you are single (and don't like it) or were recently divorced or separated, or because you have a lot of negative feelings about your relationship, partnership, or marriage. Family issues pushed some buttons, too, in this example; as a score of *D* in Thunder reveals difficulty with your parents or elders, unresolved arguments with teachers, or some other challenge with those who came before you that carries a charge. Because Earth and Thunder both got *D*'s, they go at the top of the priorities list in the order they appear. Wind, which was graded *C,* goes next, revealing some difficulty with money, blessings, and feelings of good fortune. Heaven and Fire, which you graded *B,* are placed last on the list in the order they occur. This example indicates only a small issue with helpful friends and self-enlightenment, significant enough to include them as areas to address, but less important than those that got *C*'s or *D*'s and not like those that do not need to appear on this list at all: those that received an *A*—Water, Lake, and Mountain.

This exercise requires you to make some distinctions in your life, to list in order, with some qualifications, the areas of your life that need the most attention. Your list may include all eight areas or only one—the number does not mean anything, because we all perceive our lives differently. The good news is that we can change things, and as we begin to clarify what needs changing, the priorities list helps us start to "put our house in order."

What Needs Fixing?

The list 2, 3, 4, 6, 9 means the areas symbolized by the energies of Earth, Thunder, Wind, Heaven, and Fire in your house need correction, improvement, or change. No doubt, you will need little convincing of this, because you've probably searched for a mate, read lots of self-help books about parents and children, and attended a few spiritual seminars or meditation classes before creating this list. But instead of addressing these issues directly, intuitive feng shui will show you how to deal with them by changing your environment, the space in which you live your life.

Before examining your house and learning how to change it, it is important that you reflect on each of the areas listed on your priorities list. Go through each area of your life, and visualize what you want it to look like—not just how it is. In all things, and in particular in intuitive feng shui, *image* precedes *matter*. The world of vibration comes before the materialization of the physical world, so it is extremely helpful, regardless of your belief system, to imagine how things could be and to begin practicing what it means to consider *possibility*.

The following is only an example of what you might say. Let your own words speak your truth—don't just copy a phrase from the example. Be positive—even consider the possibility of a *miracle!*

Completing the Visualization Process Worksheet

On the worksheet provided, first write the number and house you are working on (for example, 2—Earth), and then you might write something like the following:

- I visualize a good man who is sensitive to my needs.
- I can see my partner, and I begin to accept our differences and focus more on how we complement each other.
- I am attracting women who start to notice me and accept my invitations to go out. I have more choices than I know what to do with!

• I see my mate forgiving me for the past, and we start to create a future again.

Then create a space for 3—Thunder. You might write

• I notice that my mother starts to care more about my opinions and stops acting as if she's the only one who knows anything.
• My feelings of anger and resentment over what my grandfather did turn into forgiveness, and I let go of all that bitterness in the past.
• I see a change in my boss, who stops complaining and actually appreciates something for a change.

In the space for 4—Wind, you might write

• I get a raise at work and I can pay off my debts.
• One of my poems is published in a national magazine.
• Finally, I win something—for the first time in my life!
• A streak of good luck comes my way—I feel so blessed.
• Looks as though I am finally in the right place at the right time.

In the space for 6—Heaven, you might write

• I can really count on Michael—he's a great friend.
• I see the people at work start asking me how they can help instead of always turning their backs on me.
• My neighbors and I start to take care of one another—following the Golden Rule.
• I recognize that I really do have a guardian angel! Incredible!

In the space for 9—Fire, you might write

• I'm not concerned what other people think about me.
• The answers are all inside me.

• People are starting to be more attracted to me and are asking me for my opinion.

• I can begin to see that *who* I am never really dies.

Your own worksheet would contain phrases that you could imagine using if your life changed in the ways you want it to as a result of evaluating these areas sometime in the near future. They should be *I* statements, from your perspective, not "My father apologizes . . . " but rather "I see my father . . . "

Keep this list so you can make the feng shui adjustments detailed later in the book. At the very least, each area should improve by one grade—and some may even become *A*'s and fall off the list!

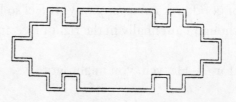

VISUALIZATION PROCESS WORKSHEET

1. Water (The Journey)

....

....

....

....

....

....

....

....

....

....

....

....

....

....

....

....

....

....

....

....

....

2. Earth (Relationships)

3. Thunder (Elders)

4. Wind (Fortunate Blessings)

....

....

....

....

....

....

....

....

....

....

....

....

....

....

....

....

....

....

....

....

6. Heaven (Helpful Friends)

7. Lake (Creativity)

8. Mountain (Contemplation)

9. Fire (Illumination)

Chapter 5

Traditional Wisdom for Modern Times
The I Ching

Understanding feng shui intuitively rests upon many foundations, but none is more important than a working knowledge of the *I Ching*. This traditional oracle is said to have been written in ancient China by Fu Hsi, the father of civilization, as long as 3,000 years ago. As legend tells us, this wise sage was meditating one day by the banks of the Lo River in northern China when a tortoise emerged from the water. In a moment of divine inspiration, Fu Hsi realized that the entire universe was reflected in the orderly markings on the shell of the tortoise.

The Eight Trigrams

The configurations of solid and broken lines, arranged in threes, reflected the macrocosm using the microcosm of eight trigrams—all the possible combinations of three solid and broken lines. These eight markings symbolized every aspect of nature: Heaven, Earth, Fire, Water, Mountain, Lake, Wind, and Thunder. Furthermore, all emotions, physical matter, spiritual qualities—everything—could be ascribed to one of the eight trigrams. From this, Fu Hsi saw the Perfect World and laid down the abstract design known as the Lo Map Early Heaven Sequence. Reflective also of the nine cardinal numbers (where the middle number 5 has no specific trigram), the pattern he created was, perhaps, the original magic square.

The Book of Changes was created by combining these eight symbols in all possible ways, resulting in 64 chapters of wisdom on the nature of change. Passed on by word of mouth for thousands of years until writing was invented, this oracle was considered the most direct link to the human understanding of our place between heaven and earth. In 1200 B.C., two royal scholars, King Wen and the Duke of Chou, amplified the verses, producing a more detailed description close to the texts available today. They also changed the position of the eight trigrams on the Lo Map, creating a Later Heaven sequence that reflected not the Perfect World in an abstract form but a world in motion—changing—with human beings at the center. Five hundred years later, no lesser sages than Confucius and Lao Tsu would spend their whole lives studying its profound wisdom as an inexhaustible source of inspiration and spiritual guidance.

Today, there are more than a hundred translations of the *I Ching* published in English, and thousands of other books and articles available, ranging from scholarly examinations of their cultural symbolism to simplistic fortune-telling guides for the market investor. Considered together with Lao Tsu's classic *Tao Te Ching* as the basis of Taoist philosophy, the *I Ching* remains a personal oracle that defies description or comparison with any other historical body of knowledge.

The arrangement of trigrams in the magic square, known as the Lo Map Later Heaven sequence, is used in intuitive feng shui as the starting point from which all design decisions are made. The "grid"—or *bagua*—is the overlay on a plot of land, a house, or a room that the architect or designer balances using basic design principles. These employ color and light, ordinary corrections of geometric ratios, arrangement of space for harmonious flow of traffic, and a number of more esoteric solutions for important areas of the bagua that the occupants wish to enhance. In chapter 7, a detailed explanation of the bagua and its use will enable you to open the door to this invisible pattern of energy.

The Bagua

Looking more closely at the Later Heaven Sequence that forms the basis of the bagua, it is possible to see a relationship between trigrams in pairs from both the physical placement and their energetic symbolism. The first "pure" pair is Heaven and Earth, signified by three solid lines ☰ and three broken lines ☷. This pair is known as the Universal Opposites. Next come the Organic Opposites, Fire ☲ and Water ☵ ; then come Mountain ☶ and Lake ☱, referred to as the Natural or Elemental Opposites; finally, there is Wind ☴ and Thunder ☳, called the Impulsive Opposites. This completes the four pairs, the eight trigrams of the bagua.

Universal Opposites		*Organic Opposites*		*Elemental Opposites*		*Impulsive Opposites*	
☰	☷	☲	☵	☶	☱	☴	☳
Heaven	*Earth*	*Fire*	*Water*	*Mountain*	*Lake*	*Wind*	*Thunder*

It is fascinating to observe that the structure of each trigram conveys a certain quality of energy closely associated with its symbolism. Heaven, made of three solid lines, is the creative force—the essential spirit from which all else manifests; exactly opposite in composition is Earth, with its three broken lines, the receptive force, open to receive Heaven's blessing as the soil receives nourishment from the sun, rain, and other forces in the atmosphere around it. Together, they correspond also to the masculine and feminine.

Examining the trigram for Fire, you can see two solid lines above and below a broken line, appearing very much like the image of a flame. It looks as if there is form to a flame when, in reality, the core is "empty." The trigram for Water, on the other hand, is made up of two broken lines on both sides of a solid line in the middle; although water appears to be clear and open, it does have mass at the center. The trigram for Mountain, a solid line above two broken lines, creates the image of space inside a container, like a cave in the side of a mountain; Lake is composed of the inverse arrangement, open on the surface, with mass below—much like a deep lake. Here, there is a distinction between Water and Lake: the former is open on both sides (like the path formed by running water) while the later is seen more from the open top, closed at the bottom like a bowl. The last pair, the Impulsive Opposites, reveals images that are again very much like their names. The roaring bass of thunder is a powerfully solid force; as it rises, thunder disperses harmlessly. The trigram for Thunder contains an unbroken line at the base with two broken lines above. Wind has no "root" but car-

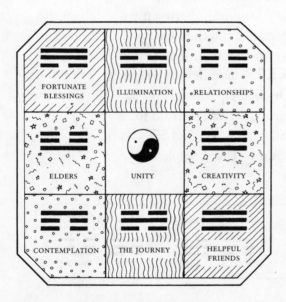

FORTUNATE BLESSINGS · ILLUMINATION · RELATIONSHIPS

ELDERS · UNITY · CREATIVITY

CONTEMPLATION · THE JOURNEY · HELPFUL FRIENDS

ries a strong force over the ground; the trigram has a broken line below with two solid lines above it.

Fu Hsi observed images of the vibrational world in relation to the elements of nature. Other symbols that correlate with each trigram serve to reinforce these associations. Heaven, the creative force, supports and nourishes all that manifests on Earth through human affairs; thus the house is called Helpful Friends. Earth, the receptive, stands for the greatest of all principles in any marriage—that of listening, receiving, and embracing everything—unconditional love. This house is aptly called Relationships. Like every other pair, the Universal Opposites depend on each other and remain connected through the vibrational world. The house signified by the trigram for Fire refers to *internal* light and clarity, and so is called Illumination;

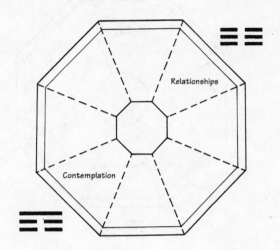

Water, flowing through time like our everyday lives, is The Journey. Fire and Water have long been related in obvious ways; in the bagua, it is through entering our life at The Journey that we can finally arrive at self-realization, Illumination. The Mountain cave is the symbol of quiet introspection and meditation called Contemplation; it stands in relationship to our joyful expression in the outer world through our offspring, and all that we manifest through this house, which is called Creativity. Thunder is like the booming voice of our predecessors, our superiors, and thus the house is called Elders; Wind is the constant flow of good fortune given by the gift of life itself; the house is called Fortunate Blessings.

Both physical and vibrational relationships exist in the bagua. Heaven is related in *image* to Earth, but *physically*, 180 degrees across the bagua, we see Mountain. Our relationships with others really emerge from our inner world; thus the correlation also exists between Relationships and Contemplation.

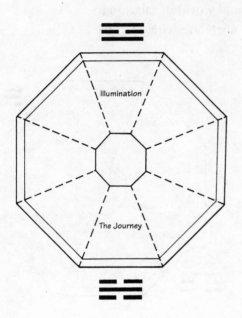

Fire and Water are in relationship through both the physical world and the world of image or vibration. Even when we achieve some fame or prominence, coming under the spotlight, what matters most is doing what we really want—honoring The Journey and its connection with Illumination.

The very *life* our parents and ancestors haven given us is the greatest of all blessings; thus the inseparable relationship between Elders and Fortunate Blessings. As we come to terms with our elders, we can much more easily realize our self-expression through creativity and procreativity, our children. The images of Elders and Creativity are always connected within our psyche.

When we are blessed with good fortune, Wind will be in relationship with Heaven; what better can we do with all that money than give it all away and live like Helpful Friends, the house directly across the bagua.

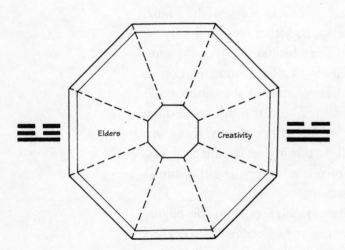

When all of these houses are in balance, powerfully related through the polarity of their physical and vibrational forces, we are said to be in a state of harmony, the essence of feng shui. This image is signified by the Tai Chi, called Unity, closely related to our overall health. Although health is often thought to be merely the absence of sickness, *true* health from this perspective means good relationships with every house of the bagua: doing what we want to do with our life (One—The Journey, Water); nourishing companionships or a vital marriage (Two—Relationships, Earth); feeling grateful and respectful appreciation for our parents, teachers, and ancestors (Three—Elders, Thunder); experiencing good luck and a sense of blessing in our everyday life (Four—Fortunate Blessings, Wind); being in good relationship with many others who support us, and giving back through philanthropy to those who need our support (Six—Helpful Friends, Heaven); sharing ourselves with little or no effort through our own, original expression (Seven—Creativity, Lake); taking time to meditate, be still and look within as we embrace the

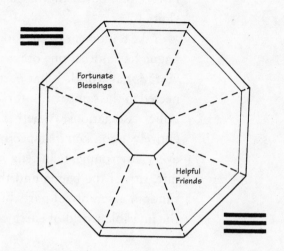

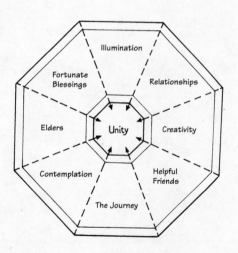

miracle of life (Eight—Contemplation, Mountain); and realizing our true, divine nature as the crown of creation (Nine—Illumination, Fire.) *All* houses of the bagua in harmony create health (Five—Unity.)

Take a moment to envision the whole. See how every house of the bagua has at least one other related house, through the physical and vibrational world. What occurs in our home and workplace is connected in the same way—through the pattern of these powerful, symbolic associations. Whether we are aware of it or not depends entirely upon our perspective and the interpretation we make in every environment. In feng shui terms, clearly demonstrated in the integrity of the bagua and the Lo Map of the *I Ching*, life is not a random assembly of parts but a *unified whole* ruled by a pattern of the invisible world of energy.

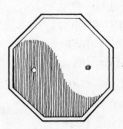

Chapter 6

A New Way of Seeing

We see very largely with the mind, and only partly
with the eyes. The phenomenon of vision depends
upon the mind's interpretation of the impression
upon the retina. What we see is not that impression
but our own interpretation of it.
WILLIAM BATES, M.D., The Bates Method

The human body is like a massive electrical power station. Our nervous system, highly developed and uniquely integrated, is the ultimate computer—reliable hard drive, lightning-fast random memory, and instantaneous character recognition. Our senses, acting in harmony, record and process data that enables us to form nearly immediate impressions about our environment.

Of our sensory organs, none is more active than our eyes. The nervous system will use billions of receptors to process information; almost two-thirds of these are related to vision. When you are "looking" for the right house, a new car, or a special someone in your life, a picture is truly worth a thousand words. And your first impression may very well be most of the story.

The easiest way to change your life may just be by changing the place in which you live and work. In the same way that it is hard for us to truly see ourselves, we cannot know what impression our house or office has on others. It is helpful to have some objective input when evaluating our environment, so ask a few different people to fill out the worksheet at the end of this chapter. See how close your impression of what you think others notice is to what they actually see and experience. Like the squirrels and owls in the trees of a hidden-picture puzzle, that which is obvious to some may remain hidden from others.

First Impressions

A beautiful painting or a vase of fresh flowers in your front hallway may be obscured by the heavily worn, stained carpet that you've overlooked for years. It may be the carpet, though, that is your guests' first impression. The comfortable armchair you have positioned in front of your desk for visitors may go unnoticed, competing with the cold, abstract marble sculpture in the corner behind you that is immediately visible to people entering your office. Intending to make the space feel warm, open, and safe for your clients, you create the opposite first impression. The fixed, powerful statement made by the art actually overshadows the more giving aspects of the furniture, causing those who visit to experience what takes place in this environment as rigid, insensitive, and impersonal.

On a hot summer day, the simple *sound* of running water in a fountain, bathtub, or waterfall gives us such a distinct impression of coolness that subjects in one study estimated the temperature in a room to be an average of 8 degrees lower than it actually was compared with the same room with no running water sounds.

What we *smell* has a deep effect on our behavior, too. According to the experience of hundreds of real estate agents, the aroma of freshly baked bread or homemade cookies will do almost as much to sell a house as a new coat of paint on the front door. Fresh lilacs or honeysuckle blossoms on the path leading up to the front door bring a smile to the faces of all but the highly allergic. By contrast, garlic, the compost pile, or the family pet may smell like home to you but most likely causes a lot of other people to gasp for fresh air.

But what we *see* is the most important of all. Patients just released from intensive care left the hospital sooner when the picture they saw each day in their room was a beautiful landscape or children playing; they remained hospitalized longer when staring at a vague picture of a tree or at impersonal medical equipment, and longest of all when given an abstract painting to look at daily.

All this strongly suggests that the images created in our consciousness, whether through sight, sound, or smell, play a powerful role in defining our experience of an environment and thus how we behave within it. We create these impressions in the early stages of experiencing an environment, and they remain a nearly indelible part of it even as changes occur and we process new information. First impressions account for more than 50 percent of the entire experience of *place.*

The exercise that follows can be used in two ways. First, take the test yourself, imagining that you are visiting *you* for the first time. Don't think—just try to feel your responses. Then, give the worksheet to four or five friends or relatives without telling them about it first. Just hand it to them one day when they visit, and ask them to play along for a few minutes as a way to support you. There is no right or wrong, so they can't make any mistakes, although some friends may try to make "safer" responses than others. Encourage them to be completely honest in their evaluations. Then, compare what your friends or family say with what you experience.

FIRST IMPRESSIONS WORKSHEET

Evaluate only what is asked of you. Circle one of the possible responses, or write another response in the space provided.

Remember: Impressions are feelings, not thoughts.

1. What is the first *thing* you saw when you arrived?

2. If you didn't know who lived here, what would your impressions on the way to the front door tell you?

3. What is the first aroma you notice in the house?

Floral Musty Wet Doggy Incense Books Shoes Cleanser Food Perfume Wood Seaside Meat

4. What patterns did you notice in the entryway?

Checkerboard Dots *X*'s Curved Lines Stars Floral Prints Spirals Straight Lines Diamonds

5. What did you hear when you arrived?

Television Kids Dog Music Electrical Humming People Talking Aquarium Traffic Heat/AC Vents

6. What did you notice here that needs fixing?

Broken Doorbell Light Bulb Out Broken Step Torn Carpet Cracked Glass (Window) Exposed Wires Door That Sticks Water Damage on Wall Loose Fixture

7. Overall, what is your impression of me, based only on what you have seen so far, responding as if this is the first time you have come here and the relationship with me is completely new?

Warm Cool Distant Serious Professional Intimate Rich Confused Busy Intense Sexy Spaced Out Creative Plain Radical Powerful Elegant Artistic Frigid Depressed Healthy Lonely Tired Open-Minded Cheap Conservative Happy Cold Worldly Cautious Innovative

8. What did you experience in the environment that caused you to circle one of the responses above?

Your Neighborhood

In some orthodox religious cultures, an intentional effort is made to conceal the beauty and ambiance of what is inside the house by making the outside look run-down, poor, and uninviting. This way of creating contrast is thought to keep the neighbors from being envious and prospective burglars uninterested.

In most communities, however, the outside accurately reflects the inside. A driveway and front porch littered with children's toys is quite likely to look like the living spaces inside. A manicured lawn and garden will most often match the orderliness of the kitchen. When considering a neighborhood, therefore, it is useful to take a close look at the houses nearby, for more can be seen than you might think at first. Healthy people and happy families usually care about the way their community looks and will make an effort to keep their homes in good shape. Take a look at your community on your next day off, and see who is out there improving or diminishing your property values! If you are considering a move into a new neighborhood, take a leisurely walk around the block and look *behind* some of those neighbor's houses. Spend some time in the local stores—buy a newspaper or loaf of bread at the corner market and stop by the local video store. These may become *your* local haunts and the people who manage them your daily contacts. How does this neighborhood feel? What impression do you have of the other customers? This short excursion can introduce you to the energy of the neighborhood better than any brochure from the local business council; it will be *your* impression, not theirs.

Arriving at Your Home

Modern building codes now dictate that the width of entryways take into consideration the possible need for an emergency exit. As a result, your front door is probably the widest door in your house. Unless you choose to be highly reclusive, the front door should be as wide as possible, inviting the world into your home. The entry should open to a clear path with no intrusion from nearby roads or buildings. Ideally, power lines should not be visible from the front door. The sill or step should be solid and stable. The door itself is best when slightly elevated. If there are many steps, they should be wider at the bottom and narrower at the top.

The hinges, hardware, and door frame should be in good working order, ensuring that the door does not stick in hot or humid weather and that the hinges don't creak. Houses where doors stick have occupants with loads of frustrations. Where shaky entry stones or creaky hinges rule, those who dwell therein become nervous and insecure.

If the door plate, knocker, or handle is of a metal like brass that could be polished, make sure it is well cared for. Doors with rusty fixtures usually lead to homes full of timeworn occupants. Check to see if the entryway is well lit at night, if possible, and that light fixtures are kept clean and free of spider webs, dead insects, leaves, or other debris. When choosing a color for the front hall, select one that is slightly darker than the rest of the house; it should, however, be well lit. Dark entryways or dirty light fixtures create confusion, fatigue, and apprehension when entering.

If your entryway is shared, as in a duplex or apartment, make an effort on behalf of the other tenants to make that part of the first impression the best it can be. Welcome mats made of strong fibers, for example, can be a pleasant and economical way to limit the dirt tracked into the building—even if they need to be regularly cleaned or replaced.

Planters or flower boxes outside the front door can very often be a beautiful enhancement; however, nothing looks as bad outside your front door as a dead plant or a huge planter full of dried leaves and cigarette butts. Make sure what *is* there is living and healthy. If a walkway leads up to the door, keep it cleared of seasonal debris like snow, dried leaves, and grass clippings. Prickly bushes, like rose and hawthorn, need to be trimmed back and planted far enough away from the path so as not to in any way obtrude on those who pass—either in sight or mind. Brushing up against a bush of thorns—even if only in the mind—makes one recoil and wince in discomfort. When planning borders along narrow pathways, choose rounded-leaf plants like ivy, other ground covers, or small flowers.

Trees near a front door should not be directly in front of the opening closer than twenty to twenty-five feet from the house. If the tree is very small, it may be somewhat closer; if it is immense, it may need to be even farther away so that energy flowing into the house is not inhibited or blocked. A tree that blocks sight of the front door from the street will block the sight of the street from the front door, too. This placement creates an excess of Earth energy for the occupants, causing their health to deteriorate. The sight of evergreens *near* the entrance, on the other hand, will add to the health and well-being of the occupants, provided the trees do not block the entry. Dead trees, or those that are badly damaged by the elements or disease, should be removed.

If the house is surrounded by a wall or fence, it should not be too close to the structure. A constant feeling of being trapped or fenced in can develop if there is too little space between the house and a border.

Pets and Other Creatures—Real and Imagined

Part of the energy of the neighborhood can be easily diagnosed by observing the animals found there. If your neighbors' bird feeders attract only black crows, or the local laundry seems to be overflowing with stray dogs, this may not be a healthy community. Take a long look at the kinds of animals, insects (butterflies or mosquitoes?), pets, and other creatures around your house. There is not much disagreement about what is more desirable—a hummingbird in your backyard or a skunk in your garbage. And though you may have little choice, at least you can become more conscious of what *is* there and make adjustments later on to improve the energy in your life by using feng shui outside and around your house.

Your Inner Voice

Finally, if you want to change the first impression your home creates, do so from the direction of your inner voice—not from what you *think* is correct, but rather from what you *feel* is right. No one says you have to have a wide door. It is simply a matter of understanding what impression choosing to have a narrow door may create—it may be exactly what you want.

And if there is very little opportunity for you to change the outside environment you already have, then so be it! Go ahead and complete the First Impressions Worksheet and move on. The key to beginning to master feng shui is learning to see the *big picture*.

Chapter 7

From the Outside Looking In

Where the telescope ends, the microscope begins.
Which of the two has the grander view?
VICTOR HUGO, 1862

Having completed the worksheets in the previous chapters, it is now time to take a look at how your house can be seen as an expression of your life and how your life is revealed in the spaces where you live and work.

Placing the Bagua

When Fu Hsi sat by the river and observed the tortoise, he set into motion the beginning of a profound way of seeing the world. King Wen and the Duke of Chou brought into view the importance of human consciousness, and with it set down the pattern of spatial arrangement called the bagua.

In reality the same arrangement as the Latter Heaven sequence of the *I Ching*, the bagua is like a grid or map we use to name and relate every area on the horizon. Beginning with our plot, drawn from the point of entry, continuing with the house, each floor and room, each desktop and horizontal surface, the bagua can even be superimposed on your face and your palm as another way to understand your life and destiny.

The method used to orient the bagua in intuitive feng shui is known as the Three-Door Gate of Chi, derived from the magic square of the *I Ching*. In order to accurately apply this method, it is essential to understand clearly which door is to be considered the Front Door. The Front Door is the main entrance, the "gate" through which energy enters your house. It will be the door used almost always by you and your visitors. If this happens to be your back door, and the door on the front of your house hasn't been opened for years, then your back door should be considered your Front Door.

You need to consider this distinction carefully. It is not necessary to use your front door in order to orient the bagua correctly if it is really "out of service." It is important to eliminate it if it is blocked by boxes or furniture or if the outside is closed off, forbidding entry. Such a door, essentially never used, is not the "Gate of Chi." If, however, the front door of your house is used very little because you find it more convenient to enter through the kitchen or from the driveway but visitors do sometimes come to the front of your house and enter through this door, then your front door *is* your Front Door. If in doubt, assume that the door architecturally designed to be your main entrance is the Front Door. This, then, will become the starting point for you in understanding how to place your plot and house like an overlay on the fixed pattern of the bagua.

Even Shapes

In a house that is symmetrical, and basically a regular shape, the application of the bagua is malleable; that is, its shape can be squeezed or stretched *as long as each area remains proportionally the same as*

70

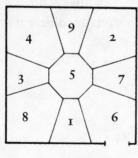

FRONT DOOR

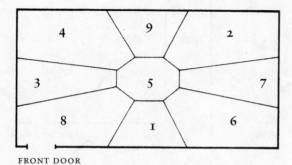

FRONT DOOR

FRONT DOOR

MALLEABLE BAGUAS

in the original. Using the shapes in the illustration, it is easy to see how the bagua can be applied to a narrow house, like a Victorian row house, a long, wide California ranch, a simple square or rectangular house, or virtually any shape of apartment or condominium unit.

The only rule in the Three Door Gate of Chi method is to place the Front Door at the bottom of the page, facing down. In this way, the

Front Door in a symmetrical house will always align directly with 8, 1, or 6. The following examples cover many different possibilities:

SYMMETRICAL SHAPES

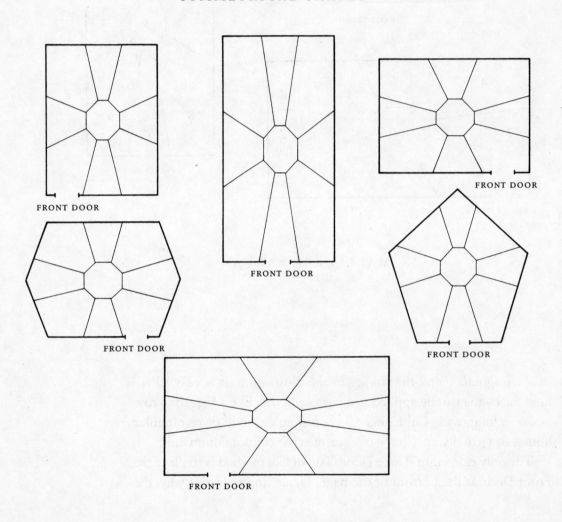

FRONT DOOR

FRONT DOOR

FRONT DOOR

FRONT DOOR

FRONT DOOR

FRONT DOOR

Odd Shapes

When the space is not symmetrical, and there is a missing corner or long extension, the bagua can still be applied, even though the door may actually enter another number. To align the bagua, place the Front Door down at the bottom of the page, and lay it over the magic square. The examples in the following illustrations show how odd-shaped houses can be aligned.

ODD-SHAPED HOUSES

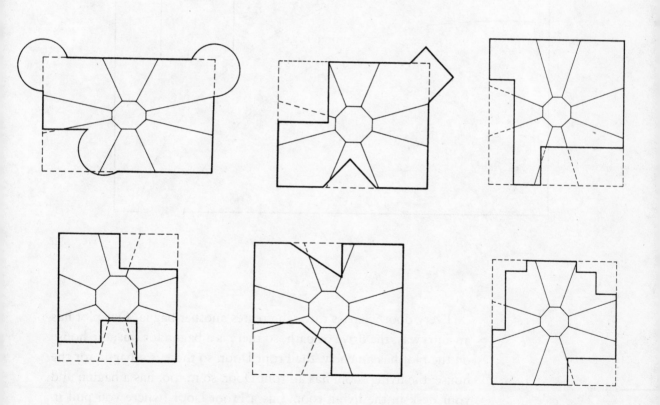

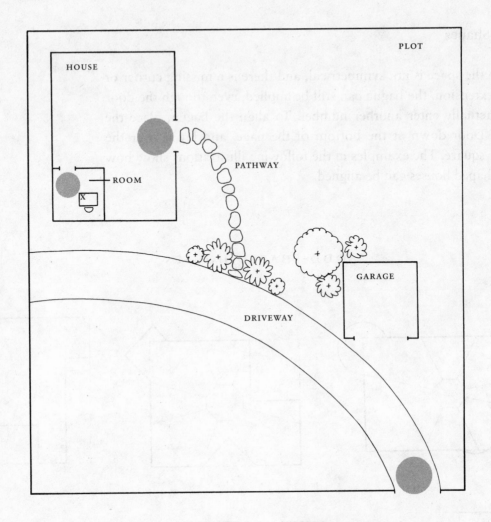

Every door we pass through creates another bagua. Our plot has an entryway, the drive or path, so there is a bagua for this; the house on the plot has an entry, the Front Door, so there is a bagua for the house; the living room has a Front Door, so it, too, has a bagua; and your desk in the living room has a Front Door (where you pull in your chair—where you enter your work area) so here, too, is a bagua. Although each doorway may enter on another plane, as in the next example, each doorway and every area will have a place in a properly aligned bagua. This has tremendous significance, because each area of the bagua symbolizes an important part of our life.

When we begin to correlate each layering, consecutive bagua, of the house, room, and desktop, we can see that certain areas of the house carry a more intense charge of one type of energy. The *X* in the previous illustration falls in the *4* area of every bagua. This area is directly related to Fortunate Blessings, sometimes referred to in classical texts as Wealth. When a powerful area like this is located in your house or office, it is possible to put some magic into your practice of *intuitive* feng shui.

CASE HISTORY

Problem: Dr. G. had been losing vast amounts of money in the stock market for nearly a year. Some income-producing property he owned had also begun to falter as tenants moved out in protest over the noise caused by construction taking place at a nearby site. Finally, a malpractice suit filed against him was making his financial woes nearly catastrophic.

Solution: After attending a weekend seminar on intuitive feng shui, Dr. G. learned how to locate the point in his house and office that related most to his difficulty with money. Not surprisingly, there were piles of bills on his desk in the area of Fortunate Blessing and minor disarray in this area in other locations at home. After clearing the specified areas, he placed a particular enhancement in each to change the energy.

Result: Five days after he completed the solution, the malpractice suit was dropped. Two days later, he was approached by the developers of the property near his own where tenants were complaining and moving out. The developers offered him a huge sum of money to sell his building so that they could expand their project. And a company in which he had just purchased a large block of stock was unexpectedly taken over by a larger company, producing a windfall for investors.

Chapter 8

Home Shui Home

There's no place like home, there's no place like
home, there's no place like home, there's no place
like home . . .
DOROTHY, The Wizard of Oz

The Bagua in the House

The most important bagua to understand is that of the area where you spend most of your time. In general, this means your house; in particular, the bedroom or the office. If you sleep only five hours a night but work ten hours a day, use this chapter to understand how to change your office, and read chapter 14. Remember, the more you begin to see how the bagua can be applied in every space, the more control you can begin to have over your life.

If you share a hallway with another tenant in your house, the bagua is sited where your own Front Door begins and does not include the shared hallway. If you live in a second-floor apartment, or on the top floor of a house where others live on the lower floors, the bagua begins where the top step meets your "ground level," which, even if no physical door is present, is your Front Door.

When trying to distinguish where the bagua for each room begins—within your house—it is not necessary to have an actual doorway. Some open floor plans for office areas at work or dining and living areas at home are divided only by a planter box or counter, leaving an opening for passage. Or, in some cases, the spaces are divided by a change in flooring materials: the kitchen is tile or bare wood and the dining area covered by a carpet. This arrangement creates a line of demarcation that becomes the Front Door for purposes of placing a new bagua over each area or "room."

Each floor has a bagua, but it is unnecessary to connect the baguas between floors. The bagua for a new floor begins where the

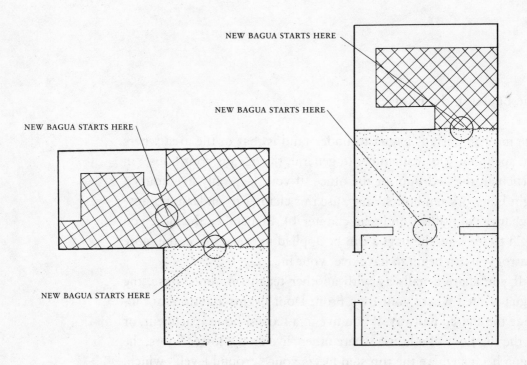

KITCHEN, DINING ROOM, LIVING ROOM

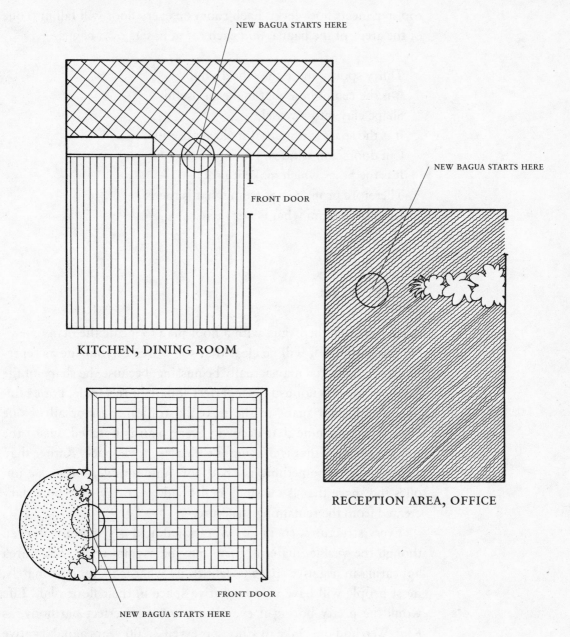

NEW BAGUA STARTS HERE

FRONT DOOR

KITCHEN, DINING ROOM

NEW BAGUA STARTS HERE

RECEPTION AREA, OFFICE

FRONT DOOR

NEW BAGUA STARTS HERE

MEDITATION ALCOVE, SLEEP AREA

top step meets floor level. Each room on every floor will fall into one of the areas of the bagua, *and* each room has its own bagua.

> Thirty spokes share the wheel's hub;
> It is the center hole that makes it useful.
> Shape clay into a vessel;
> It is the space within that makes it useful.
> Cut doors and windows for a room;
> It is the holes which make it useful.
> Therefore profit comes from what is there;
> Usefulness from what is not there.
>
> LAO TSU

Something Lost

After you align the bagua with a floor plan to locate the many possible associations, it will be clear that some area of your life as represented in the bagua may actually be missing, because the shape of the house or room is not usually a perfect square or rectangle. For example, on the floor plans in the next illustration, part or all of one "house" of the nine that occur in every plan is notched out of the whole. The area that is missing is called negative space. Rather than suggesting that something is "bad" or "undesirable," *negative* implies the space that is missing, as defined by an invisible boundary created from the remaining structure.

Every structure's energy or vibrational field is symmetrical, even though the visible, material form may be asymmetrical. Each area appearing in negative space is defined by what *is* there. Fortunately, most people will have some negative space in their floor plan. Life would be pretty boring if everything were in perfect harmony, as King Wen and the Duke of Chou observed 3,200 years ago. Negative space allows *possibility*.

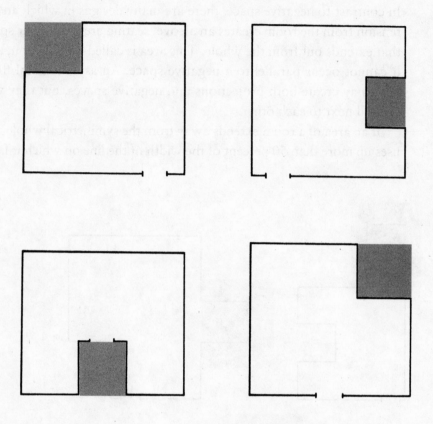

FLOOR PLANS SHOWING NEGATIVE SPACE

In intuitive feng shui, possibility is unlimited, so do not consider it a problem if you discover more than one house of the bagua missing in your home or office. Most imbalances that you discover can lead to opportunities for bringing positive changes to your environment and to your life.

Something Gained

In contrast to negative space, there are many designs in which an extension from the room creates an alcove, seating area, or larger space that extends out from the whole. This area is called a projection, and it cannot occur parallel to a negative space. An asymmetrical floor plan may create both projections and negative spaces, but they will not fall next to each other.

If an area of a room extends away from the symmetrical whole and uses up more than 50 percent of the width of the line on which it falls,

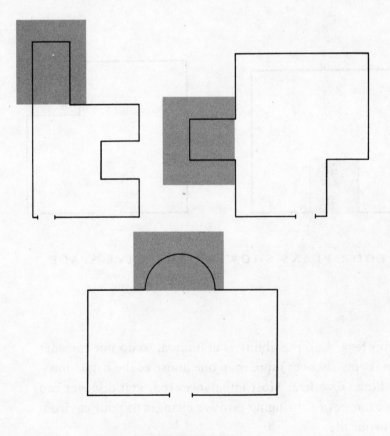

PROJECTIONS

it creates a negative space and is no longer considered a projection; however, if it is less than 50 percent, no negative space is created, and the interior area *is* a projection. The floor plans in the illustration on page 82 show some commonly occurring examples of projections.

Placing the Bagua on Negative Space and Projections

CASE HISTORY

Problem: Ms. Gabriella S. was a wonderfully creative, successful artist with many girlfriends, a good relationship with her family, and a beautiful apartment. She had been practicing meditation for eight years and felt very fulfilled and centered in her life, although she continued to search for a mate. Despite encounters with many available men, Ms. S. never seemed to be able to attract Mr. Right. After a few seminars on relationships, years of productive therapy, and countless blind dates with everyone else's perfect man, Ms. S. was still single.

Solution: Gabriella heard about feng shui from a friend who attended a workshop where the teacher drew a floor plan showing an apartment with the negative space in Earth, the house of Relationships. It was exactly like Gabriella's home! Her friend told her how to make adjustments to cure the problem, which included placing a mirror on the wall where the Earth corner was missing, and she went home to carry them out.

Result: In the week that followed, Gabriella met a man at an art gallery where her work was displayed. He asked her out, they began to see each other over the next few months, and he proposed marriage six months later. She is now, quite blissfully, Mrs. N.

Fixed Placements

There are some placements that are so difficult to cure, even with feng shui, that they should be avoided. An obvious example of poor design would be a toilet that opens directly into a kitchen, causing a mixing of two distinctly different energies. Other fixed placements to avoid for toilets are in the area of Wind (where Fortunate Blessings will be flushed away), directly opposite the Front Door (where occupants and visitors will experience the toilet as their first impression), and in the center of the house (where the energy of Water and waste could create sickness and mental instability for the occupants).

Another difficult situation is an arrangement of rooms and corridors that causes doors to bang into each other or obstruct or severely limit free passage. Doors opening into a hallway that bang into others from a closet, for example, can cause occupants to argue (their opinions may "clash") and the house to be "loud" (banging doors). These examples are fixed placements and may be costly, impractical, or physically impossible to remedy, although some approaches mentioned later on in the book may be used to lessen a chronic problem.

Fluid Placements

Where you put your bed, desk, or stove is usually a matter of choice and offers you a number of different options for arranging the space. Fluid placements can be moved and changed, and some basic principles apply.

1. *Power* and *security* come from maintaining a wide view. In any space where you sit or sleep, position furniture to give yourself the biggest view of the room and doorway. The ancient symbol of the Dragon was meant to be behind us, that is, placed for security and backup. Do not place yourself in a way that exposes your blind side, behind you.

2. The doorway is the gate or mouth of energy into the room. Do not position a bed or desk directly opposite the door, but rather slightly off to one side in order to increase the breadth of view and scope of the whole room. As little space as possible should be "behind" you. In front of you, at an entryway or door, you may choose to place some sort of guardian for protection. These symbols appear in many cultures and include lions or dogs on both sides of a doorway and religious articles mounted on the wall near the door. They are said to protect and "lift" the house to higher energies.

3. Beware of "invisible" lines of energy that radiate from the right angles of furniture at the 45-degree point. These lines, called cutting

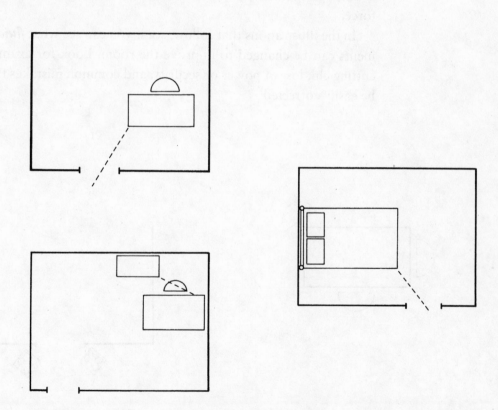

chi, intensify energy focus and cause subliminal discomfort and obstruction. A slight modification in placement can remedy cutting chi, or in some cases the use of plants or soft fabrics in front of the angle may be necessary.

Cutting chi is knifelike energy that emanates from the mass of all 90-degree angles. Because most modern structures are built with T squares, there are likely to be many such angles in your environment. Those that create cutting chi that is of the most concern will send a vibrational field out of the mass at 45 degrees into a chair, bed, or dining table where people will feel uncomfortable. If possible, place furniture in a room far away from and out of the line of this energy; if not, you will need to make corrections to disperse or soften this force.

In the illustrations that follow, see if you can see what *fluid* placements can be changed to improve the room. Look for examples of cutting chi, loss of power or security, and common mistakes that can be easily corrected.

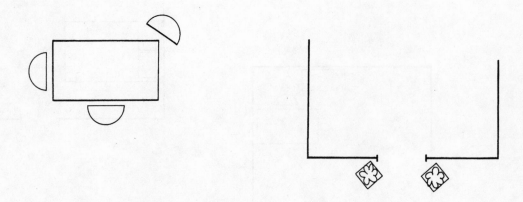

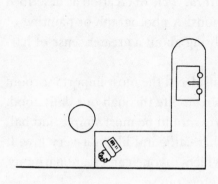

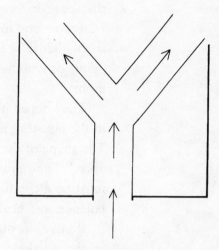

Kitchens and Stoves

Proper placement of the stove in a kitchen has always been considered one of the most important aspects of good feng shui. The kitchen, where food is prepared and life sustained, is the symbolic source of wealth and well-being in the home.

A stove placed in an island or free-standing counter is fine, providing that it is not directly opposite a sink. Water and Fire need to be balanced and apart but should not be placed in exact opposition. If a stove is sited in a corner or supported by two walls and allows an open (or partial) view of the door, the cook will feel in greater control of the space, more secure and protected. This placement is also symbolic of increasing the wealth of the occupants. Stoves should not be placed under windows or under skylights. The energy of food preparation will leave the house rather than be absorbed by its occupants.

Placing stoves next to sinks or refrigerators (fire and water, hot and cold) creates conflict and danger. To remedy this placement, common in many homes, a small plant on the counter or hanging in the space in between will allow a smoother flow of energy from water to wood to fire, along the natural cycle of creation as described in the theory of Five Transformations. A photograph or painting of plants or wood will also serve to bring about a greater sense of harmony.

The kitchen itself should be considered the most important room in the house. It is here where we create life through our daily food. The shape of the kitchen, therefore, should be most simple and balanced. The ceiling should be neither cathedral-like nor very low. It must be a comfortable space in which anyone can create harmony, balance, and health through food preparation.

If possible, place the stove so that it faces the east or light (south in the northern hemisphere, north in the southern hemisphere). Other directions are less auspicious but not necessarily disastrous. Eating areas should be calm, clear, and uncluttered with a more peaceful feeling emanating from artwork, color selection, or choice of objects.

Bedrooms and Sleeping Areas

Most of us will spend one-third of our lives asleep! Good feng shui in the bedroom means good energy when we rest. As this room is primarily for sleeping and recovering energy, colors, artwork, and other objects should convey peace. Televisions, stereos, or entertainment areas are better placed far away from the bed—ideally in a completely different room. The bedroom is best sited at the rear of a house—away from the front door—where we can retreat at the end of a long day to unwind and relax.

The proper placement of the bed depends upon many things, the most important of which is practicality. Ideally, its placement should result in easy access when making the bed and changing daily linens.

The bed should not block closet doors or passage to dressing areas or bathrooms. As in the placement of a desk, the most auspicious location for the bed is opposite the door, diagonally across from the entry in the opposite corner—not necessarily all the way against the wall—allowing for a feeling of space around the bed and a commanding view of the entire room and all who enter.

When a bed must be placed under slanted ceilings or eaves, it is a good idea to minimize the effect of imbalanced air circulation this placement causes. Occupants should install canopies or light material hung from the ceiling that covers the width and length of the whole bed, running parallel to the sleeping surface.

Side tables, headboards, and nearby furnishings such as dressers, night stands, or valets should have slightly rounded edges or be placed in such a way as to eliminate cutting chi. It is best when there is no passageway behind the head of the bed, nor should there be a large window opening directly behind or above the headboard; there may, however, be a small opening higher up on the wall behind the bed, for ventilation and light.

Most important, the lasting impression we have as we enter the "dream state" will be a result of what we see as we go to sleep. It is therefore very important that artwork, furnishings, and other accessories visible from our bedside be pleasant and harmonious, conveying a feeling of relaxation, calm, and order. To the contrary, seeing our desks piled with papers or clothes hampers overflowing with dirty laundry disrupts and negatively affects our sleeping hours.

Living Areas

In general, the living room is a reflection of our family life. It is the ideal place to display our "treasures" of art, culture, and history. It should be a comfortable, well-lit showplace where we are proud to be seen with family and friends. Seating areas in the living room should create a sense of security for both occupants and guests. Couches and chairs should be placed so that they are protected from behind. A wall, bookcase, or side table with plantings can serve this purpose. Seats that seem to float in the middle of a room, rather than being grouped together with other furnishings, should have side or end tables nearby for stability.

Chapter 9

You Are Where You Live

Your house is your larger body. It grows in the sun
and sleeps in the stillness of the night; and it is not
dreamless. Does not your house dream? and dream-
ing, leave the city for grove or hill-top?
KAHLIL GIBRAN, The Prophet

Man's character is the product of his premises.
AYN RAND, The Fountainhead

The House Defined

Every area of your house—every *house* of the bagua—carries a different energy and symbolic "charge." After completing the Self-
Evaluation Worksheet in chapter 1, you should have a good grasp of
these different areas. The purpose of this chapter is to understand
what each house means and where to locate these energies in your
own home or work environment. If you have completed the exercises
on aligning the bagua, it is now time to create the map for your life
as it manifests in your home or office. Highlight those areas you wish
to enhance, change, or adjust using the cures in the next chapter.

Symbols of the Bagua

1. WATER

The area of Water is the beginning, called The Journey.

Stand before it and there is no beginning.
Follow it and there is no end.
LAO TSU

Life proceeds along a path, like a journey. This area of our life is like riding in a boat down a river. The Water area is sometimes called Career, but it is much more than your job. It represents the freedom to do what you want to do—for life to flow effortlessly, with clarity and ease. It is a natural site to include objects containing liquid, such as inks, paint, medicine, or oil, or art that depicts or symbolizes water in some way, including rivers, streams, oceans, fish, whales, and waterfalls.

When this area is missing from the bagua in your home, some occupant of the house may suffer from illness unless it is corrected by placement. If there is a projection in this area, the occupants will usually acquire wealth and have a keen understanding of how to use it.

2. EARTH

The area of Earth corresponds to Relationships.

*I want to be with those who know secret
things, or else alone. I want to be a mirror for
your whole body.*
RAINER MARIA RILKE

Relationships with others, whether platonic, professional, or passionate, help us to become better integrated with parts of ourselves we cannot so easily see. For some, relationships with clients or customers mean money; for others, relationships are the source of great happiness, resulting in marriage and the beginning of family—for many, the main focus of life. But the essence of this area is symbolized by Earth, the Receptive. Earth corresponds to all things that receive, like cushions or pillows (they receive your body), fields and uncultivated land (open areas), and the highest nature of sincere modesty, basic humility and an empty, giving, open heart. To be in a relationship means to be truly receptive as well as giving.

The inner world of relationships is 180 degrees across the bagua, called Contemplation. Our relationships with others are always a result of how we carry them within ourselves. Earth is the area that carries the strongest charge of the Feminine Principle.

When this area is missing from the bagua in a house, women may have trouble living there. Occupants may also have difficulty with issues involving land or agriculture. When it is a projection, the house will be happiest when many women live there, although men may be much less happy in such a house.

3. THUNDER

The area of Thunder is the energy of our Elders.

If ye don't know the past, then ye will not have a future. If ye don't know where your people have been, then ye won't know where your people are going.

FORREST CARTER, *The Education of Little Tree*

Like the thunder that precedes the storm, our elders or ancestors come before us. Respect and honor for them is a traditional principle all but lost in modern society. This area relates directly to those who are your superiors, bosses, parents, and elders; some of them are in your biological family, but included are those above you in your work environment as well. Associated with energy that moves upward and outward like a tree, Thunder or Elders is also symbolized by musical instruments (noisemakers), tall plants (upward growth), sunrise, and other aspects of this energy depicted in art or objects. This area is 180 degrees opposite the house that rules children and offspring, the Lake.

When there is an indentation or a missing part of the house in this area of the bagua, occupants are liable to feel a loss of energy and lack endurance and vitality. Children born in these houses may leave home at a very early age. When there is a projection in this area, the energy created in the house will lead to greater success in life for the occupants.

4. WIND

The area of Wind is the place of Fortunate Blessings.

Should you shield the canyons from the windstorms,
you would never see the beauty of their carvings.
ELISABETH KÜBLER-ROSS

Just to be is a blessing.
Just to live is holy.
RABBI ABRAHAM HESCHEL

Most people associate good luck with winning the lottery, picking the right horse at the racetrack, or receiving an unexpected gift such as an inheritance or the prize at a raffle. The area of Wind, though often associated with wealth, is more accurately the area where we experience blessing in our lives—even in the midst of great difficulty—and remember just how blessed we truly are. Not just being on the receiving end of dollars, to be in Fortunate Blessings means to have a very real perception and experience of good luck in many areas of life, to be blessed by good omens, prosperity, harmony, and even health. Acknowledgment by a co-worker or employer, gratitude expressed by a sibling, a promotion at work, or an honor received through a trade association are all signs of Wind in harmony.

The symbol of penetration, like wind blowing through a screen, and the lighter aspects of the tree nature inherent in palms or willows are more closely related to this area and can be enhanced through art and other symbolic objects. Directly opposite Wind, 180 degrees across the bagua, is Heaven, which rules philanthropy. Of course, the more blessings we receive, the more we can give away.

When this area of the bagua is missing in the house, occupants will have more frequent accidents and experience "bad luck." They will frequently have difficulty with business affairs, documents, legal contracts, and taxes. If this area is a projection, occupants are often very successful in business and generally enjoy "good luck" and fortune.

5. THE TAI CHI

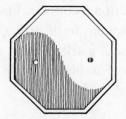

The center, called the Tai Chi, symbolizes all complementary antagonisms and Unity.

Every man is in touch with everything else, not through his hands,
though, but through a bunch of long fibers that shoot out from the
center of his abdomen. These fibers join a man to his surroundings;
they keep his balance; they give him stability.

CARLOS CASTANEDA, Further Conversations with Don Juan

The vital center of the body, called the *hara,* is the deep, rooted space from which life's energy, or chi, emanates. Like the gravitational midpoint of our anatomy, the Tai Chi in a room or house is the place of profound Unity. Here, in the center of the home, many traditional cultures and families would bring complementary aspects from the outside, like a small courtyard with a garden or atrium. Most of all, Unity must be uncluttered, clean, and orderly. More a point of reference than an actual space with certain dimensions, Unity contains aspects of all eight trigrams and may be the most important part of your home or office if your main concern is health. To be truly healthy is to unite the best aspects of all eight houses in the bagua— good relationships with friends and family, a satisfying career, feelings of being blessed, and so on. The Tai Chi contains "everything" and "nothing."

When this area is "missing," then the outside is in the inside—there is a courtyard or garden in the center! This is a wonderful design used by many traditional cultures. Placing water in this area is wise only if the water remains fresh, active, and moving. The overall dimension of an outdoor or garden area in the Tai Chi should be less than one-third of the total usable indoor space.

6. HEAVEN

The area of Heaven is the door open to Helpful Friends.

*Follow the way of heaven, reflect on the principle behind
human affairs.*
HAN FEI TZU, THIRD CENTURY, B.C.

Do as you would be done by.
FOURTEENTH-CENTURY PROVERB

The way of nature is the way of Heaven. Gifts from above, as manifest on the earth, occur in the form of support, guidance, and love
from close friends. This area, Helpful Friends, is the door through
which volunteers, supportive staff, good neighbors, and "angels" of
the figurative and real variety may enter your life. It is also the area
through which you, as a helpful friend in other people's lives, serve
by giving away your talents, time, and energy unconditionally. The
essence of this area of our house is philanthropy—not through dona-
tions of cash to a charity or tithing to a church—but through our
own selfless acts of giving away what is most important to us without expecting anything in return. It is symbolized by semiprecious
gemstones, diamonds, and lead crystal objects. Heaven also embod-
ies the strongest charge of the masculine principle, opposite the
image of Earth's feminine charge.

When this area of the bagua is missing from the house, a man will have difficulty with his employers. He may also suffer from illness and lack vitality. When this area is projected, occupants will more naturally be able to develop a concern for their fellow human beings and act in ways that support people in the society who have less material wealth.

7. LAKE

The area of the Lake is related to our Creativity.

"   "

[Be creative! Fill in the blank space provided above!]

All that we create—our children, projects, and stories and master-pieces of the art world—come from the energy of the Lake. Often called Offspring, this area of our house brings a youthful joy and imagination into being. Here, we develop plans for a new store, invent a better mousetrap, give birth to a poem or song, and plant the seed of a new life. Creativity lives in all of us, large and small, young and old. With it, life is magical; without it, life is over. This area of our house also symbolizes all the related aspects of the sensory organs: taste, touch, smell, sight, and hearing. In particular, fragrant blossoms, glistening ponds, delicious desserts, and melodious music enhance the essence of the Lake, as do images of these aspects presented in art and objects. This area is also associated with twilight, immediately before sunset.

When this part of the bagua is missing in the house, occupants will have difficulty saving money for their own enjoyment. They will tend to spend it or give it away foolishly. When there is a projection in this area, occupants will be sociable, happy, and well fed, although they may often be the brunt of ridiculous gossip!

8. MOUNTAIN

The Mountain is the area of quiet Contemplation.

To be conscious that you are ignorant is a great step to knowledge.
BENJAMIN DISRAELI

Ancient sages spent hours in quiet contemplation, often amid the clear air and quiet solitude of a mountain cave. Following hours of study or meditation, the ancients would face their worldly ignorance and deepen their knowledge of self. This area in our house, also referred to as Inner Knowledge, does not come from what you know, but instead is charged by what you know you *don't* know. A college diploma, graduate degree, or honors award in the Department of Intellect may be an important measure to some, but thousands of the world's greatest teachers, philosophers, masters, artists, and mentors drew their *wisdom* from within—and had no certification or credit from the university. Inner knowledge depends on self-reflection or introspection, often carried out late at night or in the early hours of the morning. The mountain is symbolized by containers (like caves), churches, solitary items, empty boxes or vessels, and the stillness of nature in the wintertime.

When this area of the bagua is missing in the house or is indented, a couple living there may find it difficult to conceive a child. A single woman may have difficulty with her reproductive organs. A projection in this area also leads to difficulty for the inhabitants. Family arguments and tension will abound as each person becomes more and more selfish. This is the one house of the bagua that should ideally have neither a projection nor an indentation.

9. FIRE

The area of Fire, completing the bagua, is Illumination.

Before enlightenment, carry water, chop wood.
After enlightenment, carry water, chop wood.
ANONYMOUS

Being charged by Fire means manifesting an energy of *clarity*. At the end of the cycle, as at the end of life, we finally see that light shines from within. When we are in the spotlight or the public eye, this area might be called Fame. But it is clear that public recognition or worldwide exposure can still leave a superstar in the dark. This area of the house corresponds not to being in the spotlight but rather to Illumination from within and the ability to illuminate or enlighten others. It is symbolized by the active, pulsating energy of summer and is enhanced by objects that illuminate the soul, like great works of literature, Old Master paintings, or deeply moving music or poetry. Fire is 180 degrees opposite the house of Water, reminding us that we are constantly in relationship to our path and must always be "doing what we want to do." Many people, after achieving fame and material success, are ruled by the demands placed upon them as a result of their newfound popularity. This may take them away from their path, The Journey, the house of Water—always in relationship with Fire. Many famous artists and political figures leave behind the glitter and notoriety to pursue a dream more true to their inner nature. Enlightened masters abandon desire. The mastery of Fire distinguishes human beings from all the other animals.

When this part of the bagua is missing from the house, occupants will be overconcerned about other people's opinions and find it difficult to develop self-confidence. When it is a projection, the energy that is created will often cause people to become well known in society or to achieve a state of self-realization through daily life.

Everything Is Connected

The nature of the bagua, as Fu Hsi envisioned it, was actually quite an extraordinary concept: everything in our world—all material objects, emotions, colors, occupations, spiritual qualities, seasons, and so on—could be considered a part of one area of the bagua. Nothing is left out of the whole. Everything in our lives will fall under the influence of the energy of one of the nine areas or houses of the bagua in our home.

Imagine that you are working in the mail room of the local newspaper. Although you aren't getting rich, working for a large company has certain benefits and does pay the bills. But as a hobby, you have recently taken up fine woodworking. You buy yourself a set of tools and read the trade magazines devoted to cabinetmaking. You create a few small things and give them away as presents to your friends. You soon realize that you might even make some good money by selling your work.

So, as an amateur carpenter, you decide to try your hand at building a free-standing wardrobe (armoire) and then offer it for sale in your local newspaper.

At the start of a project like this, your energy is rising like Thunder, associated with "birth" and new ideas. Envisioning, designing, and creating the piece would be ruled by the Lake, the house of Creativity; selling it would be ruled by Wind, the house of Fortunate Blessings, because a sale would result in money coming toward you.

After the first sale, you might very well become excited by the prospect of leaving your office job and earning a living designing wardrobes. This new direction in life would be ruled by Water, because it changes the course of The Journey. Because wardrobes are really big boxes, the actual pieces you create are strongly influenced by the Mountain, because physical forms like boxes relate to Contemplation.

As you get started, you find it is necessary to apprentice to a master craftsman. He or she would be ruled by Thunder, as this house also contains the energy of Elders. While working under the master's guidance, you meet another person who has been designing kitchen cupboards. This person has just started out in furniture making, and the two of you talk about beginning to work together, setting up a business making custom pieces. The association with your new partner is influenced by Earth, the area of your home covering Relationships. You discuss a few names for the new business and decide that it will be called Clearlight Furniture Design Company. A name like that would be closely related to Fire, the nature of Illumination.

The two of you need a lot of guidance and support in order to successfully market your products, but you don't have much money to go out and hire a sales representative or business manager. You know a few friends whose advice could really help get you started. They will be influenced by Heaven, the area of Helpful Friends.

These distinctions go on and on, connecting almost everything you do with all the other parts, and relating the whole to the bagua. Take a moment to reflect on what you are doing now and where certain aspects of this work fall in the bagua. Are there any trouble spots? Roadblocks? Difficulties? Each area of your life will correspond to one of the houses of the bagua.

CASE HISTORY

Problem: Lucy wrote a great biography about a famous personality from the twenties. Everyone who read it thought it was wonderful, but she couldn't find a publisher. She sent her manuscript out to many agents and editors but got back the same rejection letters and polite refusals.

Solution: After talking with a relative who had studied intuitive feng shui, Lucy learned how to locate the point in her house and office that related most to her difficulty with not getting her book published.

It was the house of Water; not surprisingly, there was a huge mess in her front hallway, the area of The Journey, where her new path would be influenced. After clearing out boxes of old junk, she tore up the carpet, painted the walls a light shade of green, and placed bright paintings and colorful hangings on the wall to stimulate and change the energy.

Result: Before the end of that week, she received a letter from a publisher agreeing to take her book. After she made additional changes, her agent called her to report that a famous actress and director wanted to buy the rights to the book for a possible project. She signed an option worth much more than she'd ever make on the sale of the book alone!

The houses of the bagua, like every aspect of your life, are intimately joined. As with holistic medicine, you really cannot approach the part and expect to "cure" the whole person. Looking at your life and living spaces, you will soon see the connection between each room, like parts of the body, and with each aspect of your life, like parts of your soul. Take a moment to look at the bagua again to see how everything is connected.

Chapter 10

Placing Changes

All changes, as well as so-called balance or equilibrium, are produced and given life by the intersecting of opposites.

GEORGES OHSAWA, Unique Principle

What Is a Cure?

Rearranging furniture in a room almost always brings a bit of fresh air into the life of the occupants. Hang a new picture, cover a chair with new fabric, or paint a wall, and you're likely to improve the aesthetic. Using the principles of balance and harmony, the cornerstones of intuitive feng shui, the changes you make in your environment will make a huge difference in your life.

In the practice of medicine, meditation, or mediation, the goal is to achieve stability near the middle—the act of bringing the focus of energy closer to the center point. Whether it is a simple cure for hiccups or the resolution of a long-standing conflict in society, most "cures" are a coalescing of opposites to create a unified whole. Even when dealing with the invisible world of vibrations, scientists know through studies that everything we cannot see or touch can ultimately be categorized as a series of wavelengths created by the material world. The angstroms of the color spectrum, the ultrahigh or ultralow frequency of sounds, and the density of materials are all measurable energies.

The association of feng shui with myth and superstition was born out of a lack of appreciation by modern people for the qualities that exist in the invisible world. For the eye untrained in assessing these energies, feng shui cures appear to be merely remnants of an unenlightened age; however, upon closer examination of most of the basic remedies used in classical feng shui, it is quite apparent that the ancient practitioner was using a principle of balance or harmony in every situation. A striking example of this practice can be seen in the story "The Little Mountain House."

In an age long ago there lived a family in a Little Mountain House. The daughter, who slept in a small room at the front of this house overlooking the valley, complained of feelings of insecurity and lightheadedness. She often thought of her path in life as being unstable and precarious.

The son, who lived in the room at the opposite side at the back, had very different feelings. Despite the love and support of his parents, he often complained of feeling confused, blocked, and depressed. Rigidity and oppression ruled his unhappy life, and few could understand why he was so miserable.

His wise parents decided to seek the advice of the feng shui master who lived in a small village nearby. When the master arrived at the house and observed the surrounding landscape, he quickly saw why the children were experiencing life in such different ways. Using the Unifying Principle, he quickly resolved the problem.

He made some simple recommendations for chi adjustment that would change how the occupants experienced the energies of the house. Behind the house, outside the boy's window, he planted bamboo. This would grow quickly and provide all of the energies opposite to the energies of the mountain. Bamboo is hollow and flexible (the mountain, solid and rigid), it sprouts quickly upward with fresh, vegetable energy (the mountain was very old mineral energy), and the plant was light and pleasant (the mountain, dark, heavy, and ominous). In front of the house, he secured long timbers and heavy stones, creating stability and horizontal energy (the cliff, a precarious drop downward, gave an insecure sensation of the vertical).

Shortly after his visit, when the "cures" were all in place, the parents began to notice subtle but distinct changes in the behavior of their children. And by the start of the next cycle of the moon, both children had become happier than they had ever been.

Where Do Cures Come From?

Most observers of the feng shui art of placement, whether they are historians, architects, or interested homeowners, assume that the cures spoken of for ages have been handed down from some wise man on a mountaintop. When feng shui is viewed as a collection of superstitious remedies, it seems to depend upon connection to some body of secret teachings.

In reality, all the adjustments used by the masters applied the Unifying Principle of harmonizing opposites. Let's imagine that the master the family consulted arrived on the scene with nothing more than a pad and pencil. Sitting behind the house, he began to make a list of the qualities of the mountain's energy that would affect the occupants living at the back. The list might have been something like this:

Down	Mineral
Hard	Still
Dark	Rigid
Old	Solid

In order for his recommendations to work, he knew that any cure he suggested must not add these elements. At first, he thought of a small fountain, because it had the elements of Water within it that were missing. But this did not seem to be enough. Then, he envisioned some flowers around the fountain but realized that this, too, fell short of the cure needed to balance this huge force. Then, he thought of planting a few large trees, which would add other elements that the fountain and flowers alone lacked. But this, he knew, would take time.

Sitting behind the house, the master made another list of all the opposites to what he'd written down before:

Up	Vegetable
Soft	Flowing
Light	Flexible
Young	Hollow

He would have to advise placement of something containing these elements in order to bring harmony to the site. It was then, after using the principle of complementary opposites known as the Unifying Principle, that he saw the perfect solution: plant bamboo behind the house. Bamboo is a rapidly growing, hollow, flexible, fresh plant that sprouts upward with new life in a very short time. The bamboo planted between the house and the mountain conveyed all its energies to those who looked outside the window, essentially neutralizing the effects of the mountain, which had caused the boy to experience life as so difficult. There was nothing unusual about the recommendation at all—it was simply the application of a timeless principle used in all other aspects of life that has worked for thousands of years.

Applying the same principle in front of the house, the master recommended the installation of well-rooted plants in solid, large vases, wide steps secured firmly to the hillside, flower boxes outside the windows overlooking the hillside planted with flora that would reveal its strong root structure, and other objects that would convey a feeling of stability, safety, and grounding missing from the view out the daughter's window. These cures helped her to gain an experience of the horizontal energy that was missing.

Understanding the Unifying Principle

Life is a series of never-ending changes. Seen through the magic spectacles of the Unifying Principle, energy can be seen as moving in and out, up and down, fast and slow, hot and cold, and so on.

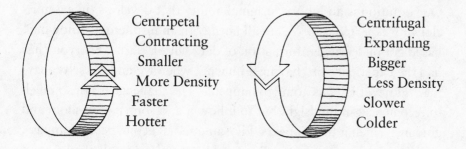

Centripetal
Contracting
Smaller
More Density
Faster
Hotter

Centrifugal
Expanding
Bigger
Less Density
Slower
Colder

Energy moving in a centripetal way contracts inward, becoming smaller and more dense. As it does, molecules begin to vibrate faster, creating friction and heat. As the temperature rises, molecules expand

and, as the principle predicts, begin the opposite kind of movement, centrifugal. The energy moves outward and becomes larger and less dense as the molecules begin to move more slowly. As energy slows, the temperature lowers until the whole begins to contract again.

This universal principle of energy has been observed as a complete cycle of change and is applicable in such seemingly diverse and unrelated fields as biology, physics, economics, and history. Using these principles to understand the imbalances present in the environment is the heart of intuitive feng shui. It is easy to see that cures do not originate from some mystical teachings of a forgotten time but are a result of sound judgment and clarity.

The Role of Intuition

There is no logical way to the discovery of these elemental laws. There is only the way of intuition, which is helped by a feeling for the order lying behind appearance.
ALBERT EINSTEIN

Our intuition is an inborn, original ability that develops (like a muscle) with repeated use. We are all born with an instinctual "knowing" based not on learned information or data but on clarity. Everyone has had the experience of "having a hunch," when we find ourselves saying, "I knew that was going to happen!" The challenge is not so much to recognize it in hindsight but to follow it as a source of wisdom and guidance when it first appears. Like an internal geomancer's compass, our intuition is like a magnet, guided by the clear, unblocked stream of energy that flows between heaven and earth along our spine. An infinite, universal "knowing" available to every human being, intuition is attracted to the opposite magnetic poles of iron molecules in our red blood cells. As we clean our blood through proper diet and way of life, our overall condition improves, allowing us to observe energy clearly, with a higher level of judgment.

Using the Unifying Principle in intuitive feng shui, the practitioner gains access to the key issue in every problem. Without it, you are watching the soccer game from behind a goalpost; with it, your seat is at the center of the stadium. It is essential to understand that intuition strengthens as a result of *internal clarity* and has nothing to do with accumulating data.

As the internal and external worlds are a reflection of each other, gaining clarity can begin from either environment. Before going on, take some time to clear the spaces you intend to "cure" with feng shui. Eliminate the clutter.

Putting Feng Shui in Your Life: Clutter and Clearing

How to Install the Cures

The cures detailed in the next section will have a profound effect on your life and destiny. How successful you are in achieving the desired results depends upon two extremely important considerations: *place* and *purpose*.

Whether you are installing cures in your home or your work environment, it is essential to maximize the transforming power of feng shui by first preparing the space. Placing mirrors or hanging crystals in a disorderly or cluttered room can have negative effects. Much like fasting or eating only a light meal the night before surgery, clearing the environment before implementing the cure allows greater positive change to occur.

PLACE

Remove all clutter from the place where you intend to practice feng shui. If you are a collector by nature, change what could be considered clutter into storage—a very different type of energy. All those bags of clothes that do not fit anymore or are out of style are *clutter*. Winter clothes you are not wearing in the summer are storage. Piles of magazines that you keep around just in case you want to refer to that article from four years ago are *clutter*. An organized collection of back issues of your favorite magazine is storage. Stacks of books and records, shelves full of tapes you never listen to anymore, and the stacks of photographs that didn't quite turn out are all *clutter* until you organize them neatly. Once you begin to look around, do not be surprised to see how much clutter you have accumulated! A relentless "spring cleaning" of your household is a good first step.

You mean to say, after all we have learned here, that
the first step of feng shui is more housework?
ANONYMOUS SEMINAR PARTICIPANT

The window sills, walls, and doorways where you might install one of the many cures should be cleared of objects, decals, and other extras. A simple cleaning will also change the energy where the cures will be placed.

You may also wish to perform a simple space-clearing ritual of your own invention or, following the example of various cultures, take a few moments to light a candle, burn incense, or cleanse the vibration of the room using a smudge stick made of sage. One ritual or ceremony is not superior to another. You are the master of your own destiny and can create the ideal vibration using your own intuition and feelings as a guide. Trust the process.

PURPOSE

When you are ready to place a cure, remember the reasons you have chosen to focus on this particular aspect of your life and environment. If it is your intention to bring into your room and life the negative space of Earth, keep this purpose clearly in your mind as you install the cure. Return to the Visualization Process Worksheet in chapter 4 and use the text you have filled in to guide you. What you create in your life will depend upon *how* you install the cure, and to what degree you allow your purpose to be embraced by *possibility*. If you place a mirror on a wall where you have identified negative space, and as you are hammering in the nails you are thinking, "This is never going to work, but what the heck—let's give it a try," you at best will have limited results. However, if you recite or see, in your mind's eye, the positive, life-changing affirmation you have written in the Visualization Process Worksheet for this particular house of the bagua that has been creating difficulty, the cure will be far more likely to achieve the purpose you desire.

In feng shui, you are not simply changing your environment, you are transforming your life. Both your thoughts and the cures carry vibration. Changing places means first changing vibrations. Remember, *image precedes matter*. Embrace possibility!

Looking glass upon the wall, who is fairest
of them all?

THE EVIL STEPMOTHER in "Snow White,"
Grimm's Fairy Tales

The Cures

Mirrors

While watching a magician saw a woman in half or make an elephant vanish in midair, the baffled spectator can hardly imagine just how simple these illusions really are. Without mirrors, more than half the magic of Las Vegas would be lost. Alice in Wonderland discovered a whole new world beyond the looking glass, and Snow White's fate was closely tied to the mirror on the wall. Because mirrors are one of the most commonly employed cures in feng shui, it is important to understand how to use them properly.

MIRRORS FOR SIMPLE REFLECTION

Mirrors have many different functions. As an ordinary object, the mirror reflects the human image and is used almost every day for shaving, applying makeup, straightening neckties or hemlines, and dressing. The two most common mirrors in our homes, in the bedroom and bath, may actually be creating difficulty while performing their basic function.

All mirrors should be kept spotlessly clean. Broken, damaged, worn, or faded mirrors will have a strong effect, usually undesirable, and should be replaced. Decorative mirrors made of smoked glass can be lovely in the right place and used in order to create a certain well-defined aesthetic feeling, but they should be avoided when the human image will be seen "amid the haze." Similarly, painted mirrors are really objects of art and should be placed so as to function as an element of design rather than reflect faces.

Because we are more than just our body or face, mirrors are frequently too small to reflect the whole field of energy that we really are. Around our physical body is a field of vibration called an aura. Whether we can see it or not, this field can be measured using various forms of technology, including Kirlian photography. The aura around the head, like a halo on an angel, extends an average of six inches beyond the physical form. When we look at our image each morning or night as it is reflected in a small bathroom mirror over the sink, who we are is limited to the physical self. Mirrors that reflect the face should be larger than the body—as we become "larger than life."

A dressing mirror should also be large enough to include more than just the image of the physical body. Occupants of a house need to be aware of their own proportions, too, so that guests who are taller or shorter do not need to bend over or rise on tiptoe to see their reflections.

Another consideration other than size to keep in mind when looking at the mirrors in your home is the mirror's edge. Because we know that they are made of glass, and their edges can be so razor-sharp that they could cut a finger if we rubbed the edge, mirrors should be either framed, edged with a border strip, or placed flush against an adjoining perpendicular surface. By doing so, we not only eliminate the obvious safety hazard, but, more important, creating the soft edge leaves only the reflective characteristic of the mirror, expanding energy, bringing more light to a corner, or creating the appearance of depth behind a counter or shelf. The cutting edge will never enter our consciousness.

Placing two mirrors side by side creates another problem. To avoid splitting the reflection with a cutting edge, use a small dividing strip of wood, fabric, or other material to mark the separation. Another option, often found in clothing stores, is to place two or more framed mirrors far enough apart so that there is at least one body's width between them. This prevents your image from appearing a third in one, a third in the other, with your "center" absent. Mirrors joined together in a corner create a strange reflection, which can be hidden by placing a large floor plant or other object at the junction point. It may be preferable, instead, to simply frame both mirrors on perpendicular walls, stopping them about twelve inches from the corner and eliminating the corner distortion completely.

Beveled-edged or etched mirrors create no problem provided that the major portion of their reflective surface is flat. The edge acts more like a frame and can add an air of elegance to an otherwise ordinary mirror.

When two edges of a mirror are on a track, one in front of the other, like the mirrored sliding doors on a closet or wardrobe or the front of a medicine cabinet, they reflect images from different depths. Standing in front of this installation each morning, the first image you see of yourself looks like the face in a Picasso masterpiece, divided in the center with the depth perspective markedly different between left and right. This creates a strong imbalance that should be avoided at all costs. Even mirrors on swinging cabinet doors, though aligned on the same plane, may have a dividing line that creates a broken image of our face—and *self*.

Small, mirrored tiles used in a hallway, living room, or dressing area that reflect the human face or form are a feng shui nightmare as they break images into hundreds of pieces. Used solely as a reflector of light to create a special effect, they can be eye-catching and full of sparkle, as anyone who has ever been to a discotheque would recall. In the foyer or front hall, they are unsettling.

Mirrors should also reflect something pleasant—something worth seeing more of, like a good view, the sky, treetops, or additional light. Placing mirrors to reflect a pond or lake into the home is very auspicious. Do not place a mirror opposite the open door of the bathroom or where it reflects the garbage can. These are tired, dead, or decomposing energies that are being removed from the house, and their image should not be reflected back into the house. In the bedroom, do not place a mirror so that it reflects your image in bed. Because our ethereal energy seeks a rest each night, such a placement can easily cause insomnia or poor sleep. It is fine to see a mirror from the bed, but you should not be able to see yourself when lying down. A mirror that reflects your body while sleeping will cause an expansion of vibrations, resulting in a subtle weakening of physical energy and an unnatural dream state. Because we are made of invisible vibrations, we are restored by the gathering together of these energies.

Mirrors in the bedroom are best when they are round or oval, creating a smoother image than those with right angles, whether square or rectangular. Circles and ovals have only one, graceful line; square or rectangular mirrors can create more conflict, especially in a small space, as the edges converge toward the corners.

Our aura, the field of vibration around us, is more spherical. A mirror reflecting our image is naturally better when it follows this form. Two intersecting lines, like those that form the corner of a square or rectangular mirror, "cross" each other in space, unlike the single, constant flow of lines in a circular or oval mirror.

THE MIRROR AS A CURE

When used as a cure in feng shui, a properly placed mirror can create the appearance of a space where there is actually only a wall. Mirrors are used to bring negative space into the bagua. When something is missing, that is, in any floor plan in which there is a part of the bagua that has no actual living space, hanging a mirror on the wall in the room at the edge of the negative space makes that area more like a projection. As a result, something that was missing in space and in life appears in both.

The house of Relationships is a negative space in this floor plan. Hanging a mirror on either of the two walls that border the negative space creates an image of something there by reflecting other parts of the room into the mirror. This cure brings in Earth, the energy symbolizing partnerships, marriage, and the receptive.

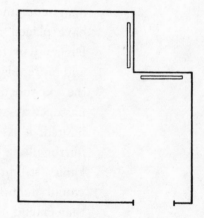

Mirrors *enable energy to flow.* Placing mirrors on both sides of the main door or entryway can bring a great new flow of energy into your life. By contrast, when a door opens into a wall, as nineteenth-century European design dictated to ensure privacy, or if a corner feels cramped, chi is stagnant and unable to flow freely—the feng shui equivalent of poor blood circulation. Directly opposite an inner doorway leading to a small hallway, or at the bottom of a stairway where the last step ends close to a wall, placing mirrors opposite

the opening creates depth. One of the most common areas where depth is restricted is the kitchen—especially behind the stove. Placing a mirror—even a small one—so that an image of depth appears rather than a flat surface will allow blocked energy to be released and open up the area with depth and light. This is an ideal cure for the tired cook who feels chained to the hot stove every day or the lonely apartment dweller who never gets any visitors. This placement also symbolically doubles the number of burners on the stove, an auspicious enhancement that strengthens health and prosperity.

In a narrow hallway or smaller space, *mirrors expand*. The little neighborhood cafe with only eight tables can appear to seat twice or three times as many customers if the owners have placed mirrors properly. Diners will feel less cramped and more relaxed as a result of the expanded image. When a passageway seems cramped or limited, it is better to place a mirror along one wall than to hang a still life painting, which would define the limit rather than extend it.

Convex mirrors have been used for decades to expand energy in this way in the entryway

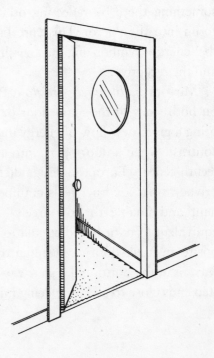

of homes and apartments. A round convex mirror is placed directly opposite the doorway. As it is difficult to adjust a necktie or apply makeup using a convex mirror, this placement was obviously chosen to spread light and energy rather than merely to reflect faces.

CONVEX MIRROR

A mirror can also be used to *define space,* as in some open floor plans. A number of mirrors along a wall, together with plants used as dividers, make it unnecessary to erect walls or other solid partitions to delineate an area. The image reflected in the mirror is expanded and defined by placement.

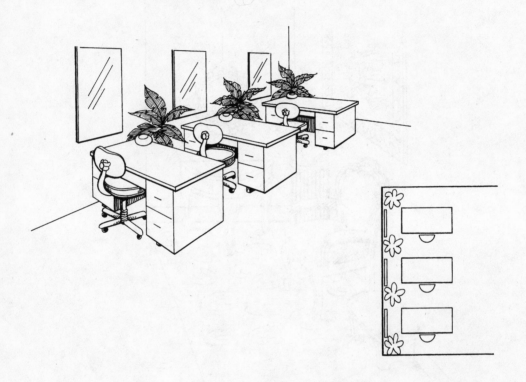

An unusual but effective use of a mirror as a cure in feng shui is when strong downward energy looms over a house, apartment, or office. The source of this energy may be a large television antenna, a skyscraper, or a water tower. The downward energy needs to be re-

versed and sent upward, harmlessly diminishing its oppressive force. Mounting a concave mirror on top of the building, on the terrace, or outside the home will invert the image, dispersing and neutralizing its effect.

Round silver balls made from sterling, aluminum, or glass will reflect energy away from a window and should be used instead of a mirror when negative or cutting chi is pointed toward the opening. The effects of sharp roof lines, corners of nearby outbuildings, or other exterior offenses, including roads aimed directly at the home or office, can be harmlessly dispersed and eliminated by hanging the ornament in the window. The ideal position is slightly above eye level at an angle of about 15 degrees.

The small octagonal mirror displaying the bagua and the trigrams of the *I Ching* is often used in classical feng shui as practiced in the Far East. It is also used to disperse negative energy coming toward the house, much as other cultures would place a God's eye, mandala, or other hex sign to ward off evil. Seen through the eyes of the Unifying Principle, all these applications do the same thing: they reflect the image back, up, and out through color, light, pattern, or other means of expanding vibration. The appropriate use of this cure depends entirely upon your aesthetic design choices and an understanding of chi energy—not on some mystical, secret powers embodied in the bagua mirror, mandala, or God's eye. In fact, using something outside your own design aesthetic may cause more difficulties. In order to practice feng shui, there is no need to make your home look like a Chinese restaurant, full of tin wind chimes and bagua mirrors, unless they harmonize with your environment or you choose them as an element of design. The principles of energy and change are not limited by culture but are present in all traditional philosophies.

CASE HISTORY

Problem: Highly cultured and refined in every way, Lady S. lived in a beautiful Victorian home full of fine antiques, both of which she had inherited from the estate of her grandfather, a former member of Parliament. Lady S. was informed by a close friend that her front door was being attacked by negative forces known as cutting chi because she lived at the top of a T junction.

Solution: Eager to correct the problem, Lady S. asked her friend for a solution and was given a Chinese bagua mirror with the eight signs of the trigrams around the perimeter. She was instructed to place this mirror on her front door. A few weeks later, not at all convinced that the problem was solved, she had become rather distressed at the effect this placement was having and sought out the advice of an intuitive feng shui consultant. Upon seeing the mirror, the consultant asked her why she had placed it there. "Well, I have cutting chi coming right in my front door," she replied, wondering why the consultant would ask such a silly question when the offensive energy was so obvious. "Yes, I can see that," he replied, "but what has happened since you have placed it there?" Lowering her voice and changing her tone, Lady S. confessed, "Well, to be perfectly honest with you, the only thing that I've noticed is that everyone who comes now asks, 'What is that thing doing here?'"

Result: The consultant then noted how completely out of character this cure was for Lady S., who was standing there in a dark blue suit, a proper, white-lace-collared blouse, and a full set of pearls around her neck. Inside the home, he found lovely period furnishings, very British in origin. He recommended that she remove the bagua mirror and in its place put a shiny, brass door knocker, convex and polished, which would both harmonize with and protect her lovely home. Lady S. was delighted at the elegant new fixture on her front door, a cure that matched her lifestyle and resonated in *her* world.

All healing forces must be within, not without!
The applications from without are to create within a
coordinating mental and spiritual force.
EDGAR CAYCE

Crystals

A sparkling crystal, a flicker of light—a rainbow of color! How magical crystals appear to young and old alike. From the earliest of times, human beings have been fascinated with the world of minerals—and why not? We are made up of millions of crystal elements, minerals in our cells, glistening deep within us like the heavenly bodies above us. Our fascination with the stars, the planets, and outer space constantly parallels our inner, cosmic search.

Crystals have an extraordinary capacity to *activate energy*. Living elements, these minerals have begun to emerge as vehicles of healing, power, good luck, and spiritual wisdom. The current fascination with minerals is hardly something new; most cultures have a deep understanding of and relationship with the earth and its elements.

In feng shui, there are two distinctly different categories of crystals, both of which may be used as cures to activate chi. The first are *clear crystals,* most often faceted, the most common of which are diamonds. Unfortunately, these are the most expensive. Diamonds are charged with a particular meaning or purpose, like love, marriage, or ideals so elevated that we characterize them as irreplaceable. Wars have broken out over such precious objects, and countless tales of intrigue, conquest, and death have accumulated in their history.

In earlier times, when kings and queens wore their crowns while strolling through the villages, their heads were in fact often adorned by a kind of traveling bagua—their presence acting as the Tai Chi. Wherever they went, *they* were the center. The eight-sided crown, with its faceted jewels of every color, served as a symbol of their spiritual power and control. The wise man, or wizard, often carried a staff topped with a round crystal, another symbol of magic over the mortal souls who sought his counsel. Today, some feng shui consultants, like the wizards of old, employ the same elements as they perform their duties.

For those with unlimited financial resources, no feng shui cure can be as powerful as a properly placed, flawless diamond to activate chi in an environment. But because few people can be expected to hang diamonds in their windows, a clear, man-made glass crystal is a perfectly acceptable alternative. Crystals on stands placed on side tables or bookshelves achieve the same results.

The glitter produced by a chandelier in the center of the grand ballroom draws us to the light. The faceted glass cover of a small candle on the table causes the flame within to sparkle and illuminate the area in a special way. A teardrop-shaped pendulum or faceted round orb hung in a window refracts the light, sending out rays of color into the room. All of these are examples of crystals activating chi.

In some cases where negative space appears, a window prevents the installation of a mirror. Instead of using a mirror, hang a crystal in the center of the window. It will activate the chi that was missing and bring it into the room and your life.

It is best to choose partially or fully faceted glass crystals that are symmetrical—like orbs, diamond shapes, or teardrops—rather than a crystal shaped like a swan or a horse, which is more an object of art. Asymmetrical faceted glass objects can create imbalance. In most cases, a small crystal, not much larger than a cherry, will be more than enough to have the desired effect. Tennis-ball-size faceted crystal balls can be used for dining rooms seating a hundred people, not ten. Immense glass crystals can cause the electromagnetic waves of light to vibrate so intensely that you might find yourself replacing light bulbs or fuses instead of activating harmonious energy in your bedroom.

Small crystals can also be installed where there is no window in order simply to activate energy in the related house of the bagua. Even the tiny sparkle they produce will draw energy into the area, subconsciously activating energy in the related aspect of our life.

The other crystals that can be used in feng shui are those made of raw minerals such as amethyst, tourmaline, rose quartz, and others. These organic minerals carry a certain charge that can be associated with the different organs, emotions, and other elements in our lives. After careful study of their properties, you may wish to use these beautiful objects as another way to affect the vibrational world. They are potentially extremely powerful, so it is important to recognize that they need to be well cared for and treated with respect. They should be cleaned every week or two in fresh water *without* salt (use of which will cause microscopic damage) and allowed to air dry, preferably in fresh air and sunlight. Much has been written elsewhere about the unusual characteristics and proper care of these types of crystals. As feng shui cures, large crystals of this type can be placed on shelves or countertops or by the bedside to activate chi in that area. Other effects are not specifically related to placement but come from the inherent properties of the crystals, which you can investigate more deeply if you are interested.

Crystals worn as jewelry affect the vibrational field around the body. When they are worn constantly, they create a certain energy and charge. With wise use, you may learn to tap into the subtle yet profound healing qualities they possess. Without knowing what effect a particular piece of jewelry may be having, however, you may be creating a subtle imbalance with a necklace or bracelet you rarely remove. Experiment with crystal jewelry, and see if you can notice how the energy of one piece may "charge" you while another may actually be draining energy.

CRYSTALS AND THE TAI CHI

It is possible to place a crystal in any of the eight areas of the bagua, or even a number of crystals in many areas. They can be used effectively alone or with other feng shui cures; however, when placing a crystal in the Tai Chi, it is wise to remove other cures, like mirrors or wind chimes, from the immediate environment, as they will create further imbalance rather than solve a problem. After many months of unsuccessfully trying various cures to change some aspect of the bagua, you can place a crystal in the Tai Chi that will change the *whole* bagua, rotating it imperceptibly as the crystal spins on its string. This is a very powerful cure and usually causes a noticeable transformation of chi in the area and one's life. It should be used only as a last resort to achieve a desired result.

The light of the body is the eye: if therefore thine eye
be single, thy whole body shall be full of light.

MATTHEW 6:22

Lights

The Unifying Principle seeks the merging of opposites. Spiritual teachers from Lao Tsu to Jesus and scriptures from the Koran to the *Pearls of Wisdom* speak of joining the "two eyes of man" into one for enlightenment. In feng shui, *light is energy,* and the addition of properly placed lighting fixtures not only changes the ambiance or mood of a room but enhances the related symbolic aspects of the house of the bagua in which they are installed.

Light can be used as a cure in many different ways. Glare, shadows, and overbright bulbs can create an unstable environment. With indirect lighting, by contrast, the fixtures are hidden but the light they create can be adjusted to fill a room. This kind of lighting may be far easier to control with a minimum of negative effects. Modern studies of emotional disorders caused by lack of light show that profound healing can take place when light is added to a dark environment. New technologies now offer full-spectrum and color-corrected instruments to replace outmoded fluorescent fixtures that cast pale, ghostly shadows in eerie hallways.

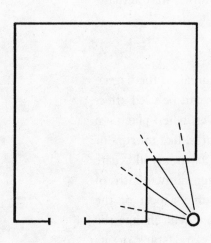

Where negative space has been identified, light can bring the missing area back into the bagua. This is possible only when the area is outside the home or work environment and the occupant is able to place a light at the imaginary corner created by the existing structure. Ideally, the fixture should be aimed so that it floods the negative space with light.

In this example, an outdoor spotlight mounted on a post or a wall can be aimed back at the house to illuminate the area of Heaven. This activates Helpful Friends, which is negative space in this house.

Fixtures positioned on the floor or ceiling close to the wall that they illuminate can be used to wash the wall with light and bring energy to the area. Up- or down-lights can be used effectively to illuminate plants, wall hangings, art, and other objects in a room. Indirect fixtures and task lighting can eliminate glare or soften an environment, or they can provide what's needed for specific purposes with dramatic results.

For most people, no light is as romantic as candlelight. White or natural beeswax candles are best suited for this purpose; colored candles may produce less harmonious environments.

Any area of the bagua, even when it is not a negative space, will be affected by the addition of light. If you wish to activate or charge a particular area, place a floor or table lamp in the house of the bagua you want to "cure," particularly if it is obviously in need of some bright energy!

Bright Objects

Mirrors, crystals, and lights are all "bright objects" and are used to add positive, active energy. Bright objects with reflective qualities add the beauty of artistic design, the softer nature of fabric as opposed to glass or metal, and the possibility of a wide range of color. These objects may be modern or traditional tapestries with small, shiny disks or sequins woven into the fabric or wall hangings made of fibers or collage with sparkling threads, foil, or specks of glitter as a part of the design. Placing sparkling objects of this type on a wall can be an effective cure for negative space or can be used to activate energy in a particular house of the bagua. Even a color or black-and-white photograph of a majestic waterfall or sparkling mountain stream can be considered a bright object that will activate chi.

Wind Chimes

Understanding that the proper placement of any object in an environment will influence the world of vibrations, occupants of a home or office must also consider the major role sound waves can play in feng shui. As one of the classical cures, a wind chime is used to *moderate or change chi flow* and mark a point where distinctly different energies converge. For example, wind chimes are often placed above the main entrance of a store or restaurant. The purpose is more than just to announce the visitor; in fact, the air current causes an audible response, subtly telling those who pass by it that "you are now leaving the traffic and outdoor noise of the city and entering the quiet, refined ambiance of our fine establishment: lower your voice and change your energy accordingly." Often positioned between the kitchen and dining room of a restaurant or home, wind chimes have the same effect of distinguishing two different energies.

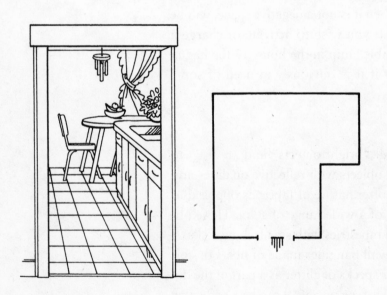

Wind chimes are available in a wide variety of different shapes, sizes, and materials as well as varying pitch, sound quality, and harmony. Because sound waves resonate differently with each individual, it is wise to listen to a wind chime or bell before purchasing or installing it. Be careful when ordering chimes through the mail; they may look far more beautiful than they sound. The correct wind chime for your home is the one that sounds right to *you*. Beauty is in the eyes and *ears* of the beholder.

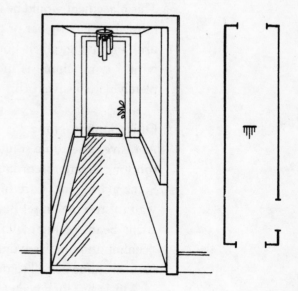

In homes where the front door is exactly opposite the back door, and the hallway in between has no obstruction or fixture to break the flow of energy, place a wind chime anywhere it feels suitable in order to moderate the flow and prevent vital life force from escaping. In long hallways or corridors, particularly where there are a number of doorways or arches, placing a wind chime in between one or more of the openings moderates energy and gently transforms one long tunnel into a few different areas of passage.

As cures used to treat specific houses of the bagua, wind chimes have a similar, moderating effect when placed inside a room. This is especially helpful when the energy of one house is disturbed or disrupted by events in life. For example, if you find yourself engaged in a family dispute with your parents or an ongoing argument with your spouse, wind chimes placed in Thunder and Earth, respectively, will help to change the energy, potentially pacifying the opposing forces.

A wind chime is used for protection from negative energy entering a home or office in two ways. The first is to install a wind chime or bell in a window facing the force, thereby changing the way in which occupants will receive the incoming energy. Unlike the round, silver ball that reflects and disperses energy, a wind chime used in this way changes it, reducing its negativity but not eliminating it completely.

This placement would be ideal when a neighbor *sometimes* plays loud music or a nearby bar or pub becomes rowdy. These energies are natural and living, albeit bothersome, so reducing or moderating them with a wind chime is more appropriate than repelling them completely with a silver orb.

Other Sounds, Noise

Abrasive, electronic sounds like that of an elevator door kept open too long create discordant energy that irritates the nervous system. Some alarm clocks are highly effective for just this reason: we can't wait to stop the noise! But when passing through a doorway breaks a silent beam of light, which in turn causes an annoying and loud "eehhnnnnnnnn," anyone in earshot would prefer a more pleasant natural chime or bell to the electronic alternative.

Music has long been shown to be an effective way to alter behavior and can be included with wind chimes and bells as an element altering the vibrational world of space. When an argument with a parent or elder persists, and the stereo system in your home is located in Thunder, it may be far more beneficial to change from discordant rock music to the more peaceful nocturne or folk song than to hang a wind chime there. Feng shui is a way of examining all things that affect our senses, so it is as imperative to be aware of the importance of music and the element of sound as it is to harmonize the world of color and light.

Both high- and low-frequency vibrations, commonly "unheard" until they cease, can cause considerable stress and irritation to occupants of a home or office. Most background noise originates from electronic devices, ventilation equipment, and ordinary appliances. Refrigerator compressors cycle on and off more than a dozen times each day; elevators hum, heat pumps rumble, and computers buzz so imperceptibly that we may not notice them until they stop! We then sit in awe of the true silence behind the noise.

Sound machines, emulating rushing water and other natural phenomena, mask these irritants but do not always neutralize them. Environments where these background noises exist can be softened by incorporating soft tapestries as wall hangings or fresh plants that absorb and balance these unnatural energies. Although the effects of background radiation have been well documented, we are only just beginning to understand how harmful the constant presence of extreme sound waves can be to our health.

Plants

There is no better way to harmonize the external and internal environment than to include plants in the interior design plan. Shape, symbolism, and sunlight, as well as color, all play a role in selecting the right plant. As a rule, almost all living plants *bring auspicious energy* to a room and help to *stimulate activity* in the associated house of the bagua. The few exceptions are culturally specific. The occupants' beliefs and preferences should be honored. Not doing so can lead to a mismatch of the ancient Chinese choices with another culture's taboos.

CASE HISTORY

Problem: Madam H., the wife of a Greek industrialist, was completing the renovation of their palatial estate outside Athens when she heard about feng shui. She was able to contact a master in Hong Kong, to whom she sent a complete set of plans. Upon receiving them back, she instructed her groundskeeper and gardeners to follow the expert's directions, which included installing a row of rubber tree plants between the main house and a reflecting pool. During the weeks that followed, her entire staff resigned, and, to her utter amazement, a large celebration she had planned had to be canceled—not only because of the lack of help but because of guests whose "plans changed at the last minute" causing them to renege on their prior acceptance.

Solution: Madam H. called in an intuitive feng shui consultant, who reviewed the plans. Suspecting that the choice of plants may have been culturally specific, he contacted a friend familiar with Greek culture. "Rubber tree plants are bad luck," he was told—a belief in sharp contrast to the Chinese position, which considers the plant to be very auspicious. Investigating the matter further, Madam H. discovered that her groundskeeper had kept this information from her out of respect, but his colleagues all had become frightened at what might happen after the plants were installed. Furthermore, the employees of the nursery where the plants were purchased had been aghast at this order from such a respectable family and began to gossip about the difficulties that were certain to befall the household. Gardeners from other households heard the sad tale, exaggerated it into catastrophic proportions, and told their employers. Before long, tall tales of grave misfortune were being whispered among the householders, each one deciding to decline the invitation to the party rather than risk bad luck by attending.

Result: Madam H. called her former staff to a meeting and explained what had happened. They removed the plantings, replacing them with flowering bushes symbolizing peace. The correction was redirected into the gossip pipeline, and a very successful, grand event was held a month later with her entire staff present and the guest list complete.

Healthy plants are wonderful additions to houses of the bagua that need strengthening or improving. They must be tended to properly, however, because if they are not they can cause deterioration of energy as they wither. Larger plants have more chi.

• Hanging plants, ivies, and creeping vines need to be well cared for, as they may appear to people as invaders rather than welcome design elements.

• The sharply pointed leaves of a palm or other semitropical plant need plenty of room to prevent their cutting energy from piercing the psyche of a person sitting in a chair or couch nearby.

- In small areas, plants with rounded leaves create less cutting chi, which can cause subtle discomfort.
- Beware of cacti in cramped areas; they grow in the huge expanse of a desert and thus are inappropriate for use in tight corners. Their needles send a subconscious wave of anxiety to those nearby.
- Dried floral arrangements, including amber-colored leaves and evergreens, are appropriate seasonally and are best avoided in the spring and summer months.
- Plastic or other artificial plants should be avoided unless there is absolutely no other alternative. In such cases—for example, where a good light source is unavailable or occupants suffer extreme allergic reactions to live plants or flowers—artificial substitutes should be of the highest quality and placed "out of reach."

A beautiful potted plant or hanging basket can transform a high-pressure work environment into a more peaceful one by contributing oxygen and negative ionization to the atmosphere. As an expression of gratitude or friendship, a lovely plant or fresh flowers are a far more positive offering than a box of chocolates!

Water

As both the literal and symbolic source of life, Water is a key element in feng shui. Our biological evolution began in salt water, and our existence prior to life in air depended upon the quality of the water environment in our mother's womb. The symbolism of Water is explored throughout this book; water as an element of design, or for use as a cure in feng shui, is particularly important to understand.

Water is *life* and should flow toward us without obstruction.

In early cultures, where placement was common sense and the need for clean water essential to life, houses were sited near good sources of water, their front doors facing in the direction of water flowing toward them. Underground energies, as well as those in the vibrational world, would therefore bring auspicious energy and vital life force to the occupants, resulting in good fortune. To enhance this energy, or to create it when it was notably absent, shop owners would commonly place a small fountain or stream near the entryway, the direction of flowing water running parallel to the path leading into the home or shop. This type of placement is frequently seen in the foyer of Oriental restaurants where diners enter.

In classical feng shui, water also symbolizes good fortune. Aquariums are commonly placed near the cash register in stores or restaurants, recommended to increase wealth.

Clear, still water can be useful in balancing negativity, where confusion and tension are present. Embodying the opposite energy of Fire, water can be used as a cure when an environment becomes too highly charged as a result of human or design elements in conflict. The cooling, passive nature of water will neutralize excess Fire energy.

In contrast, water can also *activate energy,* for example, with the installation of a small fountain or water sculpture. This can be done in any house of the bagua. A bubbling aquarium complete with goldfish is an example of a "double" cure that incorporates both the symbolism of good fortune contained in the tank and activity expressed by the live fish.

The sound of running water can also be quite cooling, as studies have shown, and helpful in an overheated environment. This is another example of excess Fire being neutralized by adding water.

Placing a birdbath outside the home, particularly if the area is a negative space, is another way to activate the missing energy. If it is not well maintained, however, the cure may create stagnation and confusion as the water becomes dirty or full of leaves. Inside installations should be kept clean for the same reason. Water placements of any type should be avoided in the northeast corner of a home.

Animals

Dogs, cats, birds, and other animals kept in the house or work environment bring in a very specific energy that is closely related to our own perceptions. A man's "best friend" can easily be regarded by others as little more than a smelly nuisance: a beautiful, rare cockatoo, for instance, might be perceived by some visitors as a source of offensive odors. Review the First Impressions Worksheet in chapter 6 to see what other people might be seeing that you are not.

Observe the symbolism related to animals in your house. If you are having trouble finding a mate and your dog's favorite pillow is in the Earth corner, you may want to find another position for Fido to call home. Animals have an extraordinary capacity to sense the vibrational world and will move toward good energy even when it is not visible. A dog or cat looking for a place to lie down outside is not just looking for the most comfortable spot but one with good chi coming from the earth. Mice who abandon a ship while it's docked at port, or who suddenly leave a house for no apparent reason, are sensing approaching danger. Many times, their departure is followed closely by catastrophe.

Domesticated animals need not be replaced by symbolic feng shui cures. Their place in the home or business environment should simply be taken into consideration on the vibrational and symbolic level as well as the practical level.

Artwork

If there is an operative principle when choosing art for the home or office, it would have to be "I don't know anything about art, but I know what I like." Whether the picture you hang on the wall is an abstract "flower" by your four-year-old or a vase of sunflowers by van Gogh, the art you select contributes to the energy and aesthetic of place as well as the symbolism and intent of purpose.

If you hang a beautiful picture of a bullfighter in Thunder, don't be surprised if you are in conflict with your parents; correspondingly, if you wish to stimulate the energy of relationships and marriage characterized by the house of Earth in the bagua, it is helpful to place there art symbolizing pairs of objects, couples, or something with beautiful imagery. Remove the single candlestick or the photo of the lone wanderer on the beach from the house of Earth, regardless of their aesthetic quality. Art is an external expression of our inner world.

The visual energy of art can have a tremendous influence on the way in which we experience an environment. To be surrounded by photographs of birds in flight, hot air balloons or kites, and tall palm trees raises our chi upward. Oil paintings of landscapes or oceans expand chi in a room. A still life or portrait tends to seem more two-dimensional and is a better choice when "depth" is intended to be internalized. Abstract and modernistic pieces without a focus will create an environment in which the occupants may find it difficult to complete things.

Wooden and metal sculptures may appear either delicate or solid and should be chosen with their symbolism clearly in mind. Sharply pointed extensions may create cutting chi and need to be placed accordingly. Their smooth surfaces, complex patterns, fine detailing, and other features will affect the way in which we perceive every work of art in relation to our lives. The way in which colors in art affect our internal and external environment is discussed in chapter 12.

Solid and Heavy Objects

Dependence upon vision can limit our ability to sharpen our other senses. It is not unusual to discover musicians or those with a highly developed sense of sound who have impaired or no sight. Many of the world's greatest composers were blind, as are a disproportionate number of piano tuners. Blindfolded, a sighted person must begin to

144

see with the other senses to compensate quite naturally for the absence of vision.

Solid objects in our environment bring energies *downward and inward*. Used as cures in a particular house of the bagua, a solid or heavy mass will "ground" what is already happening or stabilize a precarious situation. If your job is on the line, or your relationship is in doubt, placing an overstuffed armchair in Water and Earth, respectively, will help. In contrast, when something in your life is "stuck" and seems immovable, like a heavy rock, observe where in your home or workplace heavy objects may be contributing to the impasse.

Mass creates waves in the vibrational world. Standing in a room blindfolded, you can sense the difference between an immense object, like a solid, metal block the size of a piano, and a light, porous article, like a wicker basket full of feathers. Although they occupy the same space, the energy they create in waves around their physical form is very different.

It is this invisible world of vibration that first tells us that solid, heavy objects are what they are; then, using vision, we process what we "know" to be true, deepening our experience of weight, density, and other qualities by drawing from our past experience.

To train yourself in sensing vibration without dependence upon vision, try the exercise that follows.

SENSORY EXERCISE

Purpose: To help you recover your innate ability to detect the world of vibrations without the help of visual perception.

Go with a friend to a large museum, carrying with you a good blindfold that will completely cover your eyes. Take along a notebook and pencil to record your results. After you are inside, but before you enter any of the galleries, place the blindfold over your eyes, and allow your friend to be your guide, using the following list of opposites as a checklist:

_____Solid, heavy	_____Hollow, light
_____Up	_____Down
_____Live vibrations	_____Electric vibrations
_____Blocked	_____Unobstructed
_____Corner	_____Open

Instruct your guide to place you directly in a variety of places, distinguished by the quality of energy. It is not necessary to follow any particular order through this test. For example, the guide should put you in the middle of a room, where there is *nothing* in front of you, and ask you to "feel" this. Then, the guide should place you one to three feet away from a huge marble or bronze sculpture, like a Rodin or Henry Moore piece, and ask you to "feel" this, not telling you what is there. Then move on to a vase of flowers on display in the lobby, or stand directly in front of a tall plant; after that, go to an elevator door or an electrical panel and feel the energy around you.

Next, have your guide lead you to the stairway, stopping just short of the first step. The energy that flows "up" the stairs will feel considerably different from the energy that flows "down." You know this only through your visual perception, though, not through your other senses.

Finally, let yourself be guided to a corner where two solid, blank walls meet. Then, have your guide place you in front of an open window, or at a balcony, where there is only unobstructed space immediately in front of you.

Developing the senses may take some time, so don't be discouraged if you have difficulty at first in distinguishing up from down or heavy from light. As your environment (both inner and outer) becomes more clear, you will be surprised at how easy it is to "sense" what you thought you have only been seeing!

Chapter 11

How Am I Doing?

Do *not* underestimate the power of the changes that may occur as a result of practicing feng shui. The following story may remind you to explore more carefully, and with greater respect, the invisible world of energy that is affected by installing cures in your environment.

At the beginning of an intermediate course on feng shui, participants were asked to share their experiences with the rest of the group. Amazing stories of new romances, job offers, family reconciliations, and increased wealth filled the room. Most students had gone home after the introductory course three months earlier and transformed their lives with what they had learned. One man, however, who appeared quite troubled after hearing of everyone else's successes, stood up and shared a considerably different experience that shocked the group. "After the introductory weekend, I was so excited that I went right home and made a lot of changes. In the weeks that followed, my life was filled with disaster. I changed a lot of the cures, but things kept happening that seemed to come from what I was doing. One of my children fell down the stairs and broke her arm; our refrigerator compressor froze up and needed to be replaced at huge expense; my wife had a brief affair, I was laid off from my job, and there was a small fire in my workshop. I came back to this course to find out what I did wrong and how to get back my normal life again!"

With jaws dropped, other participants questioned him about what adjustments he had made. He went over the long list of changes, including hanging crystals in windows, placing mirrors and wind chimes, painting walls, moving furniture, replacing artwork, and installing cures that he had invented. He admitted that he'd neither cleared the space nor paid attention to the visualizations, but this was not the reason why things had gone so wrong. One student finally asked him the right question: "What was wrong?" "That's just it," he responded quickly. "My life was great! I had a good job, a happy marriage, healthy children, a good income. I thought things would get better!" An old woman jumped to her feet. "If it ain't broke, don't fix it," she yelled.

The man in the example was "changing" success and happiness to its complementary opposite—failure and misery. The installation of one or two carefully placed cures will improve even the happiest, most successful life. Just go slowly if you are already close to where you want to be, and don't overdo it! Feng shui can have powerful results, like many other practices, if approached recklessly or without respect for the invisible world of vibrations.

Evaluating What You Have Done

Here is where the priorities list you created in chapter 4 can be quite useful. Address the areas of concern you have in your life with these priorities clearly in mind. Don't be greedy about money, for example, if you have a pretty good cash flow but simply want more. Chances are that changing a related area, which reveals far greater difficulty, will also improve other parts of your life. Getting into a good relationship leading to marriage might double your income!

Move slowly, placing only one or two cures at a time. In this way, you will be better able to evaluate the cause in relation to what is happening. Hanging mirrors or crystals all over the house may change things, but it will be very difficult to trace the source cure. If you happen to make a mistake and place a cure incorrectly, a small problem may arise that will tip you off to the error. If the mirror is put in the wrong place first, a major catastrophe will not occur, nor is it likely that things will improve.

Is It Working? How to Tell if the Energy Is Changing

Small improvements should become apparent almost immediately, and at the latest, after one full phase of the moon has passed, about thirty days. Reflect at that time on what you have noticed. Has one of your poems been published after you placed a plant in Water? Have you become pregnant after hanging a crystal in Lake? Did you break through a logjam in your relationship with your dad after hanging a mirror on the wall bordering the negative space of Thunder? Through simple self-reflection, see how your life has changed.

In the months that follow your first successes, continue to move slowly through the priorities list until you reach the end. There should be a cure or adjustment installed for every house of the bagua where you have identified problems, imbalances, or difficulties in your life and space. Any area you gave a *B, C,* or *D* needs attention, but begin with the more difficult challenges.

When Things Get Worse

One of the basic laws of the Unifying Principle tells us that, at the extremes, everything changes to its opposite. A balloon will expand continuously until it bursts. A country's power will grow until it collapses. As we approach the end of a long cycle of change, things may get a bit worse before they begin to get better.

If you are certain that the adjustments you have made are correct, and you have checked and double-checked the guidelines in earlier chapters, do not remove a cure if something appears at first to get worse. The rejection notice will look better in hindsight if the next publisher accepts your poetry and wants you to sign a contract for more money. Missing a boat that sinks is a blessing, although it is hard to see that when you are left stranded at the dock.

After a while, if things are clearly not improving despite your best efforts, look *within*. Answers to chronic problems are usually right in front of us and easily overlooked. It is more likely to be something incredibly simple than something extremely complex. The next part of the book can broaden your understanding of feng shui and the many related areas of practice that can make a difference in your life. Don't give up—your relation to your environment can be seen on many different levels.

The Predecessor Law

One of the most important principles to understand in feng shui is the Predecessor Law: the overall vibration that remains in the space from those who lived there before you dictates much of what may be happening. It is beyond your ability to change through ordinary means of installing cures and studying the bagua.

If you move into a house where the previous occupants were divorced, and where the couple who lived there before that were always in conflict, then the chances that you and your mate will have difficulty are disproportionately higher than the laws of averages would predict. If the company whose offices were in the space in which you are now working had serious financial troubles that ended in bankruptcy, then the space still carries this energy, making it difficult for your business to succeed.

On the other hand, if the store you are about to rent was vacated by a booming business that was forced to move to a larger location to expand their growing business, the space they leave behind carries an energy that is very auspicious for success. And if you and your new spouse see a house where a couple lived happily for twenty years raising two healthy children from birth until they left for college is now vacant due to their move to a smaller home, buy it—the Predecessor Law suggests that it is an ideal environment in which to raise a happy family.

In the next chapter, on controlling chi, you will learn what forces are present in your life that can change the energy of an environment. Without even knowing it, however, many homeowners discover that what is happening in their lives is a repeat of circumstances that may have taken place years—or even decades—*before* they moved in. Most of what has occurred will be clearly in evidence in the structure of the house. Negative space in Earth, without correction, creates an absence of the energy needed to create and support harmonious relationships. A toilet in Wind causes a loss of the energies of good fortune, that, without correction, will lead to grave financial difficulties. In other words, you could be flushing your money away.

Stories of haunted houses, attic spirits, and jinxed storefronts can be easily understood through feng shui. Similarly, tales of guardian angels or houses with good vibes are examples of harmonious environments where the feng shui is most auspicious. As much a study of the invisible world of vibration as it is of the physical world of structure, the feng shui of any environment must be investigated deeply. When you discover problems that stem from the predecessor, there are ways to correct the imbalance.

Treating the Invisible

It is very likely that all you need to do to correct an existing effect will be very apparent after you look at the bagua. Many homeowners have installed mirrors or lights to correct negative space when the problems of the previous tenants could be clearly related to difficult circumstances. The familiar restaurant site that seems to change owners, and cuisine, every six months can be corrected by ordinary feng shui cures. Even very large buildings, like offices or hotels, can benefit from relatively small alterations in design by using the very basic precepts of feng shui.

CASE HISTORY

Problem: A famous hotel in a major metropolis was unable to keep the occupancy rate high enough to turn a profit. The owners refurbished the guest rooms, created a new marketing plan with a top advertising agency, and hired a number of high-level managers to run the property. After three years, little had changed on the bottom line, so the owners decided to put the property up for sale. It was purchased by a group of investors who were aware of feng shui and saw a golden opportunity.

Solution: The new owners wasted no time in making only one correction. They changed the placement of a pair of escalators that directly faced the front door. In the old design, the chi went straight down the stairs and out the door, an inauspicious placement that symbolizes loss of fortune. After the renovation of the entryway, the escalators were positioned at a right angle to the door, with a pool of water at the bottom. Energy was now blocked from rushing out— the experience of the predecessor—and was furthered strengthened by the additional cure of contained water.

Result: The hotel recovered from its financial difficulties and now enjoys one of the highest occupancy rates in the city. The new owners have profited enormously, their renovation costs repaid tenfold in the first two years.

If disastrous events have taken place in a home prior to your living there, it may be necessary to perform a simple but effective ritual to change the existing vibrational pattern. This process can be performed within the context of almost any religious practice as a complement to your personal beliefs. It is not intended to replace or negate any other method but to be used as a method of self-reflection and purification.

Clearing Spaces

Our dead never forget the beautiful world that gave them being. They still love its winding rivers, its great mountains and its sequestered vales, and they ever yearn in tenderest affection over the lonely hearted living and often return to visit and comfort them.

CHIEF SEATTLE

In the late evening or very early morning, when the vibrations of society are at their lowest, take a place in the room or area of your home where you feel the "presence" of any spirit or where you sense the most discomfort. If you are unaware of such vibrations, then position yourself in the Tai Chi of the house or any main room other than the kitchen.

Sitting on a cushion or pillow on the floor, or in a chair, make your back straight and relax your shoulders. Close your eyes gently, and quiet down your mind, letting go of the many small details you carry around each day. Allow thoughts like "I have to pick up the dry cleaning tomorrow" or "I must buy more paper towels" to pass through your consciousness without attachment. Let the ordinary sounds of refrigerators, clocks, and traffic come and go. Focus on your breath as it enters your nostrils and again as it leaves. Do not force anything to "happen." Simply allow yourself to be still and quiet as you would in a basic meditation practice.

After a few moments of stillness, take a deep breath in through your nose, and as you exhale, make a simple tone or chant by expressing the sound "suuuuuuu." This should come very gently, without forcing, causing your throat to vibrate slightly. Continue to let thoughts come and go, and pay no attention to the constant commentator inside your head. Repeat the sound three or four times, with each exhalation.

With the next inhalation, return to a regular pattern of breathing for a minute or two, sitting in silence. Slowly, begin to see, in your mind's eye, words and images that you can speak aloud or think. Either way, you will be operating within the world of vibration as your thoughts and spoken words function through wavelengths.

In cases where there was a loss of life, think or say something like the following:

> Thank you very much for your life. If you have been in this house before, or were the person who built this house, thank you for what you have done. We are grateful for the beautiful masonry you made around the fireplace and the wonderful oak tree you planted in the backyard. For everything that you have done, for your many years of life here before me, from my heart I offer my thanks.
>
> Wherever you are now, I wish you well. In the spirit world or the world of vibration, although I may not fully understand where you are or what happens when we leave this world, if you are there and here now, I hope you can be happy. May the space you are in bring you peace.

Don't worry about us—we will take care of this house now. There is no need to stay here anymore. We promise to take care of ourselves and our family, so you are free to go now. There is no need to hang around in this space that we have now occupied, so you can freely go on and feel at ease with what will take place here. We will seek to make ourselves happy and healthy without your presence. Take care and go in peace.

The exact words or images you use are not important and should be tailored to fit any circumstances about which you may be aware. All that is essential is that you perform this ritual from your heart. You may combine a prayer from your religion, or chant a particular sutra from another teaching, or read an appropriate passage from the Scriptures, if you choose. It is a very simple communication with a place "beyond the veil" that exists in all our lives. You need not think of it as special or all that unusual, as you are already operating very much in the world of vibrations through the practice of feng shui. This ritual simply includes a purification for a living spirit, clearing the spaces of the vibrational world much as we clear clutter from our attics. But in this case, because the problems of human lives are being addressed, it must come from the heart in order to be effective.

Sit for a few more minutes in quiet meditation, and allow the images you have created to remain. As they diminish and when more mundane thoughts begin to appear, extend your arms in front of you, and clap your hands together very sharply three times, making the loudest sound you possibly can. Doing this will clear the space further, and more completely, at the end of the ritual.

When you have finished, take a very small handful of sea salt and spread it around the room, throwing it here and there without "aiming." Salt, as it is the most compact, dense ingredient we use in our everyday cooking, and can be considered one of the most important elements of life, is the exact complementary opposite of the invisible world of spirit or vibrations. Using salt in this way helps to balance a space where spiritual phenomena dominate the physical world. By spreading salt, you clear the space and balance the visible environment with the invisible world. Let the salt remain for a few days, and whenever you feel it is appropriate, simply sweep or vacuum it up. At a later time, you may wish to scatter the petals of fresh flowers around the room and light some candles to initiate a new vibration into the space.

You can easily invent similar rituals to fit different circumstances, wishing prior occupants well and pacifying or neutralizing any negative charge that remains from the predecessor. The important thing to understand is that we must become aware of what has taken place before in a space in order to avoid having catastrophe repeat itself.

The following story is a stunning example of the possible consequences of ignoring the invisible predecessor energy. It is only one of many documented cases; difficulties abound in areas where people have died unhappily.

In World War II, on a particular site in Russia, a bomb dropped by the Allies hit an orphanage, instantly ending the lives of hundreds of innocent children. Following this tragic event, the space was never "cleared," nor did anyone perform any type of ritual in order to free the area of the presence of "spirits" or energies trapped in this world of vibration. Years later, the government used this site to build an important structure that would provide the region with electricity.

It is known as *Chernobyl*.

Because feng shui originally emerged as a practice to honor the spirits of those who lived before us, it is only logical that we must acknowledge the possible presence of this world where we live or work. A simple prayer or heartfelt blessing is often all that is necessary to release negative energies we may not even know exist.

Chapter 12

Changing Places

*Your sense faculties give you access to possibilities
of deeper perception. Beyond ordinary perception,
there is super-sound, super-smell and super-feeling
existing in your state of being. These can only be
experienced by training yourself in the depth of
meditation practice which clarifies any confusion or
cloudiness and brings out the precision, sharpness
and wisdom of perception—the nowness of your
world.*

CHÖGYAM TRUNGPA, *The Sacred Path of the Warrior*

Changing Perceptions

Feng shui is strongly dependent upon *perception*. If we feel, see, taste, or touch something, an interplay between "us" and "other" begins to take place that we evaluate through the many parts of our nervous system. Changing the environment that surrounds us changes our perception of it, whether that change occurs in our consciousness or not. Few people "sense" the quality of energy in the air in a room with a negative ion generator. Most people do feel that the room is more clear, relaxing, stable, or energized, or they simply feel a bit better in this room than they do in an identical room that does not have an abundance of negative ions.

A white shirt, to some people and cultures, is a symbol of purity; to others, it is a symbol of death. Black may be a color of mourning or sadness for some; it may be a strong indicator of fortune for others. Aside from the cultural and societal conditioning with which we were raised, many other elements affect the way we perceive the world. Seen dogmatically, feng shui can appear to be nothing more than just another set of beliefs. Used as a point of reference for the individual, it cannot be considered apart from the many other factors that affect our chi and the energy we perceive through the millions of neurons in our physical bodies.

As biological beings, we are affected physiologically by color in many ways that are built into our central nervous systems from birth. But there are also learned behaviors that influence how color affects us personally. Some hospital workers cannot tolerate green tablecloths, since green reminds them of the color of their surgical gowns, often bloodstained at work. Others have early childhood associations with one or more colors that last a lifetime. These cultural realities play a large role in how we relate to the whole world of color.

What Controls Chi?

The single most powerful and important controller of chi in our world is ourselves. We are not just a bag of bones and tissues ruled by certain limiting "scientific" constructs such as calories, gravity, or other conceptual dogma. After observing a demonstration of *chi gong*, the traditional Chinese exercises to develop chi, most people clearly see that it is possible for each individual to train in one of the ancient martial arts and direct energy in ways that might seem unimaginable. Superhuman feats of strength, balance, resistance, concentration, and extrasensory perception are common among practitioners of these arts. Arising from many years of practice, these abilities confound scientists, whose laws of physics offer no explanation. Practicing feng shui leads to understanding how to control chi.

We control our own energy. By embracing a way of life that honors the very real world of invisible vibration, we can change our diet, exercise regimen, and activity in order to change the quality of our perception. The ancient Chinese, Indian, and Tibetan masters recognized the importance of diet and its relation to health; we in the Western world have only recently begun to acknowledge that. As diet and meditation practices begin to be recommended as a cure for heart disease, modern scientific research validates what has been known for thousands of years.

It is difficult to imagine using feng shui to change the external environment without addressing our own personal internal environment: the body and mind that give us the perception of the world in which we live. By changing the quality of our blood through a change in diet, we begin to change the very way we see the world. Our brain cells, bathed constantly by the blood we make from food, give us the vision of our everyday life. In addition to an awareness of diet, a meditation practice or similar training that is designed to free up the clutter in our brains rather than add more muscle to our body helps us to begin experiencing just how much control we really have over our lives. Although diet and way of life are often the most challenging elements for most people to change, it is essential to recognize the inherent limitations of feng shui adjustments in the external world absent of changes to ourselves within. We are not separate from our environment, nor is our environment separate from us. Positive changes made within together with feng shui adjustments in our external environment profoundly expand possibility.

Other People

Next to ourselves, the second most important thing affecting us is *other people*. Though we may be whistling a happy tune as we arrive home, we cannot help but be influenced by the energy of a depressed mate. In particular, our relationship with our parents is of profound importance because it essentially defines the way we will experience other men and women in the world. Any therapeutic methodologies, be they psychological or spiritual, that can lead us to the inescapable recognition of who gave us our life are worthwhile. Developing a deeper sense of gratitude and appreciation can begin to free us from the stranglehold of the innumerable stories and interpretations we have created of our lives. The biological and spiritual in our life form an inseparable bond of energy that occurs with no greater power than in that between parents and children.

So, to more deeply understand the transforming power of feng shui, we must also look inward, to ourselves and our own lives and energy, and to our immediate relationships with others, particularly our parents. Wind chimes and crystals hung in exactly the right places may increase the possibility of changing our perceptions through the change in our environment, but we would be wise to remember that self-development begins within and will really only be supported by what occurs in the external world.

The Importance of Symbolism

As the wise old man on the mountaintop tells the seekers who appear before him, life itself is meaningless; it has only whatever meaning we choose to give it. For the world-class tennis player, all that matters is the trophy and the winning payoff; for the grandfather, it is the photograph of his first grandson catching a striped bass; for the bride-to-be, it is the wedding ring; for the politician, it is the pen used to sign a document. Each object carries with it huge symbolism. What matters most in our life is what we *say* matters—not the pen, or the ring, but the significance we give the object in our minds. Behind the obvious lies the world of symbols.

When Fu Hsi watched the tortoise emerge from the river, he saw everything falling within one of the eight energies of the bagua. In the physical world, all our material possessions such as artwork, furniture, clothing, cars, houses, photographs, pets, collections, and so on—everything—can be seen as symbolizing one of the eight basic energies.

If we are looking for endurance in our relationships, for example, a photograph of a bunch of bananas is far less appropriate than a picture of a pine forest. Instinctually, although we may not consciously perceive it, we know that the pine trees are always green and will last for many years. The banana, on the other hand, will rot in a few days unless we consume it; and in either case, it won't last long.

Symbols in our home and work environment are everywhere. Their impact must be considered in feng shui when we seek to make improvements in our life. Using the First Impressions Worksheet in chapter 6, review your space as others see it. If you are trying to find a mate or improve your relationships, look for that single candlestick or lone pillow on the couch in Earth and replace it with paired objects. Is there an abstract painting hanging on a wall in an area where you really want focus? Does your dirty laundry pile up in a corner related to that part of your life that's giving you trouble? Does your door stick, entering through a correspondingly "stuck" house of the bagua? It is truly astounding to discover how the realities of your life manifest everywhere in symbols. Changing these energies means bringing in the symbols you want.

Designing Your Own Cures

Where there is cutting chi, there is an angle that creates a sharp "point" that must be corrected. Placing a round object, like a potted plant, or soft material like cloth or ribbon over the corner will balance this energy. When too much metal or stone is in an environment, for example, a kitchen with marble countertops and steel appliances, adding light, straw baskets, or soft flowers warms and opens up the energy of the space. In these cases, a simple application of the Unifying Principle is all that is needed.

Some rooms have low-hanging ceilings or heavy beams in which there is a strong downward energy. While a bamboo flute may be used in classical feng shui to lift chi upward, many other possibilities exist that will have the same effect. The reason the flute is placed, mouthpiece down, at a 45-degree angle underneath the beam is to give the impression that it is being used as a sort of brace, the wind passing through the flute lifting chi upward, thereby neutralizing the downward energy in the room. But in some environments, a bamboo flute is hardly an appropriate design element.

With the Unifying Principle, one can easily see that it would also be possible to place a large, reedlike plant, growing tall within the space, to achieve the identical effect. Other cures for the same problem could be a photograph of a colorful hot air balloon sailing above the sea, a gaggle of swans in flight as they take off from the ground, or a child throwing handfuls of confetti into the air at a party. All of these carry the energy and symbolism of lightness and upward energy by conveying a meaning and feeling experienced within. These cures are equally as effective as the classical ones and are even more powerful when you invent them yourself.

Colors

The visual spectrum of colors as refracted from sunlight spread into varying wavelengths measured in what are called angstroms. The longer wavelengths, red and orange, create intensity and command attention through our eyes. These more vivid, hot colors have also been shown to create activity, as the matador knows very well. Colors created from shorter wavelengths, like violet, are more passive or cooling; their effect in an environment is calming.

Appearing as early as the fourth century B.C. was a system of classification of energy known as the Five Elements. Translated more accurately today, the terms used to describe the movement of energy in this system might have been The Five Energies Going, as it implies movement through a continuum rather than a collection of static elements. A color is associated with each energy, but it is helpful to explain the system of these elements, called the Five Transformations, while looking at the related colors.

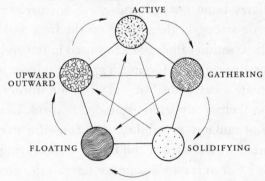

FIVE ENERGIES GOING

THE FIVE TRANSFORMATIONS

The energy of Water, our evolutionary and biological origin, is *floating*. Like the stillness of the late night or very early morning hours and the winter season, the inactivity of this energy is associated with difficulty or calamity, as when water becomes stagnant or cloudy. The related colors are *blue and black*. Actually the absence of color, black absorbs other colors, and if used excessively in design, will create a depressing environment. Its best use is in definition, as a border or accent color edging or framing other colors. Too much black in a room will diminish physical energy quickly and can cause a lack of clarity; just the right amount can lead occupants to greater precision. In the psyche, black plays the role of the shadow figure, the character hidden from our conscious, waking thoughts. We have a lot to learn from this part of ourselves, but we can easily be overwhelmed by its projected influence in daily life. The use of black in the design process, like that of other colors, needs to be very carefully considered. Like their element, Water, both blue and black are extremely important to use in appropriate amounts.

Water nourishes the next energy, Wood, which moves *upward and outward*. Wood energy is not "hard" like a tree, but rather is moving similar to the energy of a tree. It is associated with the early morning, the spring season, and the color *green*. The predominant color of the vegetable kingdom, green signifies growth. Its wavelength stimulates bone growth and good posture. In most cases, green also has a strong healing effect on the liver and gall bladder, stimulating the creation of bile, which is used in the body to emulsify fats in the digestive process. Too much green in a room, other than in plants, can create a naive idealism, its vibration uprooting the occupants, moving them away from grounded realism. Used more delicately, green stimulates possibility, affecting the nervous system much as a parent would affect a child when encouraging them to "go ahead and try." Green is only *becoming* active—moving toward fire, but not yet fully charged.

Wood nourishes the next energy, Fire, which is *pulsating, active* energy. Fire is associated with midday, when the sun is overhead, the summer season, when nature is very active, and the color *red*, the most highly charged wavelength in the visual spectrum. Using the color red in the design process will stimulate activity that, if excessive, may create great difficulty for occupants. The use of red in prisons or mental hospitals, for example, has been shown to create violent behavior, causing residents to become more excitable and emotional. Large, vivid patches of red in curtains, upholstery, or carpeting excite the mind and can contribute to migraines, impatience, and general anxiety. Red is seen infrequently in nature, appearing mostly in times of heightened activity, another indication that red carries a strong charge. The proper use of red can induce passion and sensuality, stimulating the sexual libido. It is no coincidence that certain districts in urban areas are distinguished by a red light.

Physically, red will strongly excite the digestive system, accelerating the process of fermentation in the stomach. Open wounds or sores take longer to heal when exposed to red light, as blood takes longer to coagulate. As an aid in food preparation, a red cloth draped over bread dough, homemade pickles, or sauerkraut, for example, will accelerate the fermentation process. In the home, parents of young children should be careful not to use too much red in their children's rooms or clothing, as it may overstimulate a small child. In contrast, for more mild, fair-skinned children, it may prove to be quite helpful. Red is like fire: both positive and harmful energies are present. Handle with care!

Fire turns into ash, creating and nourishing the energy of Earth, the *gathering* force of the soil. As the energy moves inward and condenses, Earth brings nature to fruition, as we do at the end of a day. The harvest season, also referred to as the late summer, is the time of Earth and is further associated with the color *yellow,* moving inward. The use of yellow in an environment stimulates occupants to become more aware of the gathering of energies, promoting socialization. The yellow rose, long associated with jealousy, can be very soothing if used as an accent rather than the primary part of a floral arrangement.

Less intense than red, yellow can be said to be more inspiring than stimulating, as its wavelengths are more closely attuned to the intellect and society. Much has been written to suggest that yellow was the favorite color of Socrates and Confucius, among many other philosophers. This color motivates individuals to consider their relationship with the masses, drawing introverts out and reducing the likelihood of introspection. In the West, yellow was rarely used in religious ceremony. The White House landscapers could have a considerable effect on the government were they to plant more yellow flowers around the perimeter of this power center. Its energy would begin to gather a stronger, social force around the president through the vibration of wavelengths yellow creates.

Finally, Earth hardens over time into the energy known as Metal, the force of *solidification*. Metal is the end of the day, and year, when the autumn season appears and nature prepares to turn inward. Metal is the culmination of the cycle of transformations of energies and is associated with the color *white*. In healing, there is no purer color available than white, as it is in reality a harmony of all colors and wavelengths. White fabrics, flowers, and clothing suggest purity and refinement, an unfortunate association that probably led to the bleaching of whole-grain flours, which strips them of their nutrients. White bread has artificially added nutrition, necessary after it has been refined. This process, called enriching, is truly one of the most oxymoronic practices of the "civilized" world. The cowboy with the white hat, always the "good guy," is another product of our obsession with purity. The dastardly villain, dressed in black, is instantly associated with evil. Society must work very hard to overcome these deeply rooted stereotypes as they have trapped us in so much unconscious prejudiced thinking.

FIVE COLORS

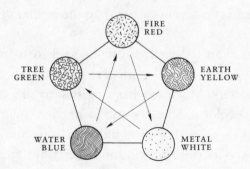

The Five Transformations are created by a *cycle of creativity* or nourishment moving clockwise through the five phases. Each energy is dependent upon the one preceding it, in what is referred to as the parent-child relationship. Water is the parent of Wood, Wood the parent of Fire, and so on. Within the creative cycle is a system of checks and balances called the *control cycle*. In this internal system, each energy controls the child's child, or grandchild, and is controlled by a different energy, the parent's parent.

Water controls Fire; that which is very active must be kept in check by a still hand. One of the many different ways in which we can see the five transformations in life is in anatomy and physiology. In traditional Chinese medicine, the Fire energy of the body is the heart, while the Water is ruled by the kidneys. We know in physiology that it is the kidneys that regulate blood pressure—a demonstration of Water keeping Fire from raging out of control.

Wood controls Earth, the former's upward, outward movement balancing the soil's tendency to gather too much and become hardened. Fire controls Metal through "melting," Earth controls Water by "absorbing," and Metal controls Wood by solidifying energy that may move too strongly up and out. The whole system has brilliant symmetry and serves as a cornerstone of the theoretical structure on which the ancient philosophy from the East is based.

Colors in harmony will occur in the cycle of creativity, or nourishing cycle. Red with yellow, for example, conveys a strong active, gathering energy (as apparently at least one fast-food chain knows very well!). Red alone with white is not nearly as attention getting. Green and red together are powerful, whereas green and yellow conflict somewhat and move our chi up and out and down and in at the same time—and eventually nowhere. Add a splash of red to tie them together, and there is the possibility of more movement. Green controls yellow.

In feng shui, as in nature, the more intense colors are used sparingly, more as accents, or when consciously creating a certain effect.

The center of the spectrum, green, can appear within our homes in the form of plants with only a moderate effect of moving energy upward, symbolizing growth. Too much red in a preschool will cause children to bounce off the walls with hyperactivity, as studies have shown. Violet may pacify an office environment, causing drowsiness, but may be the perfect choice in a room where tranquillity is desired. In commercial enterprises where money is the primary concern, violet is as far away from materialization as we can move before we cross the line and become "invisible." Although violet or purple may be the personal preference of a business owner, their use in the interior design of offices is not likely to increase profits. Stronger colors help to manifest things in the material world.

Where a calmer environment is more desirable, as in the bedroom, large red curtains may be contributing to insomnia. If it is just a splash of red in the bedspread, in a few flowers, in a picture or a work of art, this is less likely to occur. Dark shades like gray or black may create depression or neutrality, in either case lacking any real definition unless used in combination with stronger colors. Using gray in schoolrooms or government offices makes these environments very boring.

QUANTITY CHANGES QUALITY

A well-known axiom of the Unifying Principle is important to remember when considering the use of color. Each individual will perceive the vibration produced by color differently. Our physical and emotional states are changing constantly, together with our preferences. As a child, your favorite color, like your best friend, probably changed quite frequently. But it is the quantity of any one color that matters—the amount affects the quality of our experience.

Rooms where the overall color scheme is orange or yellow will benefit from a splash of red here and there; too much red will overpower the environment, intensifying the vibration. A touch of blue or violet in the same room may have little or no effect; these cool colors must be used more generously to achieve any result.

Intense colors attract our eye—especially when they are placed in contrast to milder ones. Too much of an intense color, like red or orange, could have the opposite effect. Black can be quite dramatic, used properly; it will be heavy, or even somber, when there is no contrast. In an environment that uses some of almost every color, the eye cannot distinguish one from the other and becomes almost blinded. Each of the five energies has a uniquely different effect and must be used to create a comfortable flow of energy—designed to achieve a particular purpose.

> The five colors blind the eye.
> The five tones deafen the ear.
> The five flavors dull the taste.
> Racing and hunting madden the mind.
> Precious things lead one astray.
> Therefore the sage is guided by what he feels
> and not by what he sees.
> He lets go of that and chooses this.
>
> LAO TSU

COLOR WORKSHEET

The following practice test is designed to help you better understand the proper use of color in feng shui. Refer to the text in this chapter if you are not sure of the correct answers. Once you have completed the test, you will have a basic understanding of the principles discussed in this section.

1. A woman with a pale yellow love seat in her living room has decided to purchase two or three small pillows to be placed on it. How would the colors she uses affect the furniture? What colors should she avoid?

2. You have just received a dozen red roses from a secret admirer. Checking your china cabinet, you find no glass vases—only one that is royal blue with black edging and another that is made of a creamy white china. Which one do you choose? Why?

3. You work in the sales department of an automobile dealership, and sales are off this month. The boss offers you a choice of two new chairs for your desk to replace the old folding one you have been using—a black leather chair and another covered in forest green fabric. Which one do you choose? Why?

4. The new Chinese restaurant that just opened in your neighborhood is decorated with red walls. What kind of energy would you expect to find there? Explain.

5. You are throwing a party to celebrate the merging of your company with a former competitor. Their president's secretary, who has been appointed to coordinate the event with your approval, hands you a list of supplies for the black-tie affair. The tables will be accented with colorful centerpieces. They are open to your suggestions. Any comments?

6. Your daughter has broken her leg while skiing and is in traction, laid up in a hospital. She says she needs a new nightgown to wear—the one the hospital gave her isn't very comfortable. What would be your first color choice?

7. Your children, who spend a lot of time together in the playroom in the basement, always seem to be getting into arguments when they are in this room. What would you look for, and do, in relation to color to change the situation?

8. The copy writers at the advertising agency where you work aren't feeling very inspired these days. Checking their open-plan offices, you find a symphony of color everywhere, with no one hue in clear command. Any suggestions?

9. The small powder room off the entry hall has black-and-white checkered tiles on the floor. Your mate asks you to choose some new guest towels to be used there. The local bed-and-bath store has only pale green, bright red, or canary yellow, all with black piping on the edge. Which one would you choose, and why?

ANSWERS

Colors are more than just a matter of personal preference. Your choice of colors, patterns, textures, designs, and materials all affect human behavior in any environment. Though it is not necessarily "right" to choose one color over another, certain colors will help you to achieve harmony and balance, and others will create conflict and discordant energy.

1. Using white on the pale yellow love seat would create an energy of "settling down." Using red or orange would activate the user more. She should avoid pure green, blue, or purple as they conflict with white unless there are additional tones to harmonize them.

2. Roses in a royal blue vase may be elegant to some people, but the strong blue will diminish the red of the rose. The flowers will be uplifted (with their intended romantic energy) if placed in a vase made of white china.

3. Black, the absence of color, diminishes energy. A green chair will get you up and out, encouraging a rising energy.

4. Red walls in a dining area activate chi—sometimes too much. Although there may be a lively, talkative crowd in the restaurant, excessive energy in a dining area may be counterproductive to healthy eating. Appetite is overstimulated and strong stomach acid is produced.

5. Look to see what the new corporate color scheme will be and display it prominently. If there is an opportunity to use yellow flowers, the energy of gathering earth, it will help support the merger.

6. Green will help her bones to heal more quickly. Avoid blue or purple when structural problems are present.

7. Too much red or orange or vibrant "neon" colors in a playroom can cause hyperactivity. (Cutting chi might also be present!)

8. Creative energy is flowing in an ad agency and needs curved lines of color to support it. Try to harmonize the area with blues and greens, like streams of water and growing plants, with only the occasional splash of vibrant colors. Reduce blacks, grays, and washed-out colors.

9. Pale green is a quiet color and may make a small powder room seem peaceful but dull; red is "classic" in this combination and could make the room feel very elegant. Yellow is the weakest choice, as there is the least contrast for balance. But the right answer—the only answer for all of these—is to choose the color you feel is the best—because you say so!

Chapter 13

When the Magic Works

Inch by inch, row by row, gotta make our garden grow,
All it takes is a rake and a hoe, and a piece of fertile
ground.
DAVE MALLET

Take It Slow

As you change your perceptions of the world around you through
feng shui, more and more of what you already know begins to be
confirmed by your experience. Belief is replaced by certainty, doubt
by possibility. The magic can happen so quickly that it may be difficult not to get carried away by the immensity of what using feng shui
could mean in other parts of your life.

Sharing the Secret

There is an old story about Mahatma Gandhi, whose courage, common sense, and inspiring view of the world affected millions of people.
One day, a mother brought her young son to meet the wise old man.
"Kind sir," she began, "my son will not stop eating candy. He is ruin-
ing his appetite and his health. Because he knows of your wisdom,

would you please tell him to stop?" Gandhi quickly replied, "Please come back and see me in two weeks." The startled mother took her son and left and, as instructed, returned two weeks later. Gandhi smiled upon seeing them again and, kneeling down, looked right into the little boy's eyes. "Young man, please do as your mother asks. All these sweet things cannot help you to be strong and healthy." Gandhi rose and stood proudly before them both. Bewildered, the mother asked, "Why did you have us return after two weeks? That is what I wanted you to tell him then—I don't understand." "Two weeks ago," he replied, " I had not stopped eating candy myself!"

Beyond just practicing what you preach, using feng shui in your life will give you a greater appreciation and respect for other people's lives. If you really want others to benefit as you have, you are likely to have a far greater influence as an example of positive change than as another proponent of an unheard-of system.

Improving on a Good Thing

Instead of racing through your environment seeking to cure all ills, continue by going further with what you have created. Clear *more* clutter from Earth *after* a new mate shows up. *Re-pot* that old plant you moved into Heaven to expand further your new relationships with a supportive friend. *Maintain* the sparkling crystal you placed in Wind, even though the blessings are already flowing, by keeping it spotlessly clean.

Also, look at both bigger and smaller baguas, and make other changes in the same house of the bagua but in different settings. For example, if you got a new job after clearing the clutter and placing a cure in Water in your house, look for the Water area in your new of-fice, find it in your bedroom, and locate the spot on your plot that correlates with this energy. If you do not clear all three of these areas, too, or others that carry the influence of Water, the results may be only temporary, like a remedy in medicine that does not treat the cause of sickness but only the symptoms.

You might also begin to ask yourself *why* Water has been stagnant in relation to your body and health, which you can better understand after using the information on feng shui in the body presented in chapter 15. What steps can you begin to take from the *inside out* that will further strengthen the new direction your life is taking?

So when positive results begin to be apparent, the most prudent approach is to both broaden and deepen your horizons, expanding into related areas like health and related astrologies and delving deeper into the philosophy of feng shui as it is expressed in the *I Ching*.

A New Reality

If you don't know where yer at, you can't see where yer goin'.
WILL ROGERS

If you return to the Self-Evaluation Worksheet in chapter 1 after changes brought about by installing cures have become evident, you will be able to reassess your life and see just what has really happened. Reviewing the affirmations and priorities list from chapter 4 a month or two after you first created them may seem like reading old notes from your private journal. How you felt about your job, relationships, and life in general is likely to surprise you, because the positive changes that begin to occur after practicing feng shui greatly affect your perspective. A story shared by a successful consultant helps to illuminate this point.

Robert was a single professional who loved Harley Davidson motorcycles. He owned two bikes, one with a sidecar for a friend to accompany him on his frequent, weekend outings. Robert had all the Harley regalia; his black leather jacket, key chain, pen and pencil set, cigarette lighter, and T-shirts all carried the official insignia. Everywhere he went, Robert met others who shared his passion; he encountered Harley aficionados at the post office, outside theaters, at local restaurants, and in the office building where he worked. He attended meets, exhibitions, and weekend outings dedicated to the culture of motorcycling. But most of all, it seemed that everywhere he looked, there were Harleys.

Eventually, Robert fell in love with a woman who shared his passion, and they spent their leisure hours biking into the back country in search of life's many adventures. Soon, Robert proposed (while on his bike), and she accepted (embracing him from behind), and they were married. Not long after their honeymoon, she announced that she was pregnant and that her doctor had recommended that she curtail her cycling until after the birth. Undaunted, and tremendously happy about the prospect of becoming a father, Robert continued to enjoy the world of Harleys on his own, always the faithful husband and father-to-be. The nursery was soon outfitted with all the basic necessities, and their house and hearts were filled with love. Still, everywhere he went, he saw Harley Davidson motorcycles.

They were blessed with a new son, a future cycle enthusiast, to be sure. Shortly after the birth, Robert boarded his bike to spread the news and hand out the traditional cigars. But a funny thing happened. Everywhere he went, at every stop sign and toll booth, in front of the post office and at work, he noticed *Volvo station wagons.* Strapped in the backseat of every one was a child's car seat. Harley Davidsons totally disappeared from sight, and Volvo station wagons began to pop up like daffodils in the spring. Red ones, black ones, old ones, new ones. To his utter amazement, they were everywhere.

Considering that there'd been no massive recall of motorcycles that month, nor anyone giving away free Volvo station wagons, Robert realized that the world hadn't really changed at all—*he had changed*. The invisible, subconscious images forming deep in his nervous system told him that his world had now become the world of the family, that transportation needed to be safe, that motorcycles and babies don't mix, that the quiet, reliable protection of a sturdy car—with space for a stroller and diaper bags—was the *new reality*. Harley Davidsons disappeared from the world of his unconscious imaging, and in its place was a totally new paradigm. How the world occurred to him, his vision and perspective of everyday life, had been altered by external changes on the physical plane.

When the changes from feng shui begin to occur in your everyday life, you will be creating your own new pattern, different from what was there before; furthermore, this pattern will change the way you see the world—and there is nothing you can do to prevent it. This process is very much like the old children's puzzle: You are shown a pretty picture of a forest. Somewhere in the trees, there is an owl, a snake, and a butterfly. As you look at the drawing, you see nothing but trees, leaves, and flowers. You cannot believe that these animals are in the picture! "Look very closely," says your friend, or, "Don't try so hard to see them, and they will appear!" Finally, after you stare at it for ten minutes, the owl's shape comes into view—and then you see the snake! A few seconds later, the butterfly shows up on a leaf, sitting right there in the middle of the picture!

What you can no longer do is look at this picture *without* seeing all three animals, although only moments before, you would have been willing to bet good money that they were not even there. Your reality has been changed by the appearance of something unexpected. Soon, you take it for granted, and there is no turning back.

Removing and Moving Cures

Because of the impressions this type of experience makes on our memory, a pattern of experience emerges. Then it becomes very difficult to change these old patterns permanently. After you see how much your life has changed as a result of installing feng shui cures, you may actually want to make the phone *stop* ringing with job offers or suitors and may need to remove a cure. If you do, be certain to have in your mind an appropriate visualization to direct your life toward the way you want it to be.

Don't add clutter to cancel the effect of a cure. Don't try to change your front door in order to "shift" your bagua. You will always have the power to create your own life and reality, and with a little bit of practice, you can adjust the effect of the cures as easily as you turn down the volume on your stereo. Feng shui *evolves,* and with it, your experience will change.

If you should decide to move and are concerned about affecting the cures from which you have already benefited, go slowly. Look at the bagua in your new home or office, and you should be able to easily see what needs to be done. Each space is very different, although the floor plan may be exactly the same. Dimensions, colors, textures, patterns, orientation, and location all affect the internal bagua. Any space you choose will integrate with your life in a slightly different way—on another frequency or another vibrational level. As you become more confident, moving cures in the same environment, like rearranging furniture, will become a good way to improve the flow of vital energy in your space and in your life.

Chapter 14

Feng Shui at Work

I am too smart of a businessman to ignore some-
thing that has been around for three thousand years.
ANONYMOUS BILLIONAIRE INDUSTRIALIST

The Changing Workplace

There are now hundreds of inspiring books and innovative seminars and workshops aimed at changing the way we conduct business. Corporations and nonprofit organizations are clamoring for new ways to sell their products and services; management and labor, strongly influenced by the emerging powerhouses of their Asian competitors, are rewriting contracts, discarding old labor systems, and reinventing the workplace. Catalog sales and money-back guarantees empower consumers, while in-house health centers, concern for work-related stress, and sensitivity training improve worker efficiency and job satisfaction. Over the last decade, change has come so quickly that a company's success depends most of all on moving away from "business as usual." In nearly every industry, information equals power, and innovation spells profit.

One unfortunate effect of this massive shift can be seen in how far away many work environments have moved from the natural world.

Buildings with windows that do not open provide "fresh air" through high-tech ventilation systems. Computer work stations surround employees with pulsing electromagnetic charges. Cellular phones held inches away from brains receive ultrahigh waves, strongly affecting the nervous system. Plastic plants adorn lobbies that have artificial lighting. Copy machines, furniture, and building materials emit toxic gases that slowly erode health. And overtime, late shifts, and sales quotas disrupt the natural rhythms of the internal clock.

There *are* ways to reduce these unnatural forces and neutralize their debilitating effects. In some countries, legislation has brought about a few changes such as installation of radiation screens on computer terminals or limitations on overtime in high-stress jobs. But even these changes came about long after most people's common sense told them they were necessary. It took years-long studies and political pressure to get the job done.

New disciplines are currently emerging that examine geopathic stress, "sick building syndrome," and other environmentally caused illness. Research in such fields can help people interested in these important phenomena learn how to improve the workplace. In addition, you yourself can use the principles discussed in this book to make your work environment a more healthy and harmonious space, benefiting others who work with you, too.

What You Can Do

After your next weekend break or holiday away from the place where you work, go in on Monday morning with a copy of the First Impressions Worksheet from chapter 6 tucked away in your briefcase or knapsack. In the same way you evaluated your home—from a place of "emptiness"—fill in the worksheet for your office, store, or workplace. Also, if possible, ask a few friends to do the same thing, as you did for your house. Then step back from the process, and take an objective look at the results. Could you detect a marked difference in noise levels? Were you (or your friends) aware of any unusual vibrations such as those caused by spinning computer hard drives, cycling air conditioning, or humming electrical machinery? Did you sense any change in air quality? Are there other aspects of the environment that appear to be unhealthy? Simply becoming aware of what you may have been taking for granted all this time is the first important step.

Next, create a bagua grid for your office, plant, or shop, and notice where the houses fall. Determine the negative space and projections, and see how existing circumstances may be influenced by either of these. Look at the wall colors, desk shapes, and artwork. Is there too much warming energy? Is there cutting chi? Do the images and symbols of photographs or graphics depict what you want to create there?

Discuss with a co-worker a little of what you have learned from changes in your own house, and see if you can come up with suggestions that you might offer your employer or office manager. It may be necessary for you to buy the full-spectrum light bulb or new plant for the office if your boss is "not interested" or there's "no money in the budget." Considering you spend a quarter of your life in this environment, it will prove well worth the cost and effort to make these positive changes. In many ways, the place you work may be as important as your bedroom!

Your Personal Space

Offices are meeting, gathering, and working areas, reflecting the energies of earth and metal in the Five Transformations. In order to assure an even and balanced sense of energy in your work environment, first make certain that the lighting in the whole office feels harmonious. Use task lighting for individual areas, but be sure that the room does not look like a space full of spotlights.

Get your desk or work station in order. Get rid of clutter, and organize your files. Your desk will be a reflection of your brain and intestines. Move the waste bin out of Wind.

Organizing systems that are more horizontal than vertical are more appropriate when there is a feeling of too much work. Stacks of letter trays in an office can make you feel the piles of work are endless. Take that pile of papers and other junk that's been sitting in Fortunate Blessings, and put it in order. In its place, put a beautiful crystal, a vase of flowers, or a new plant. Make Earth appropriate for Relationships. A favorite photograph or beautiful object is a better choice than unanswered correspondence or overdue invoices. Go through every area of the bagua and consciously choose what you want to go where, adding cures wherever you feel they are needed. Remember to follow the guidelines on how to best install effective cures.

The shape of your office will foretell the nature of the work supported within. Square offices, or those in rectangles slightly larger than a perfect square, will make the most money. Irregular shapes, like *L*'s or overlong rectangles with corridors or extensions, make an environment where completing projects is more difficult. Triangular offices, or the use of triangular or diamond patterns on furnishings or carpeting, create conflict and reduce cash.

Ceilings in management offices should be higher than those in support offices nearby—not the other way around. Do not hang light fixtures, plants, mobiles, or other objects over desks. Skylights directly over desks, unless they are very high overhead, disperse energy in the work environment.

Placing the Desk

The ideal placement for a desk is so that it is opposite and in the area furthest away from the door. Ideally, it should be backed up by a solid wall rather than an open window, creating a corner where energy can gather. In the best of circumstances, this area should be the house of Wind, Fortunate Blessings.

The desk should be placed parallel to the wall rather than at any uneven angle, which would create a feeling of conflict in the room. It should also not be placed too close to the corner, which could create a feeling of limitation. Like a bed, it should never be placed in front of a mirror (you will have twice as much work)!

There should be no passageway behind an executive's desk, nor should there be any strong artwork placed on the wall behind the desk, as it will distract visitors. Strong artwork, calendars, photographs, diplomas, and other wall hangings may be placed in any other area of the office.

Desk Size, Shape, and Surface

Your desk should be large enough to allow both a work surface and available storage area and small enough so that everything is easily within reach. A desk that is very large may be impressive but can easily reduce your efficiency. A desk that is too small can lead to frustration.

Square or rectangular desks, or those with right angles and sharp edges, are more appropriate for commercial enterprises where *making money* is the first priority. Curved, oval, or round desks are better suited for environments where *creativity* is the first priority. When both material success and creativity are of equal importance, choose a desk that combines graceful lines with defined, square edges, being careful not to create cutting chi with the corners. The corners can be cut in a radius.

The surface of your desk should not be too strongly reflective, as it will quickly create eye problems and fatigue. Black desks or desks of other colors that create high contrast will slow you down. You should be able to see "into" your work—it should neither bounce off the desk nor disappear on the surface. Desks for any purpose should be balanced and symmetrical and convey a feeling of organization and calm.

The Telephone

Aside from the computer or word processor, your telephone is probably the most important electronic fixture in your office. The ease of its use depends a great deal upon proper placement. Make certain that cords are well concealed and, in particular, that the coiled line between base and headset does not cross your work surface. When you talk on the phone, try to make certain that your spine stays straight, opening a channel between heaven and earth for clear communication and energy to flow. Cradling the phone on your shoulder bends your neck and spine, accelerating fatigue and blocking chi.

If you use a cordless phone, keep the base off your desk, replacing the handset in the unit only when it needs charging at the end of the day. In this way, you can keep a cordless phone handy according to your needs. Mobile phones that contain both receiver and transmitter in the handset place you at great risk for excess electromagnetic radiation—its effect on the central nervous system is implicated in suppressed immune function. If you are accustomed to using a mobile phone, do so with the utmost caution, and try to use it only when absolutely necessary.

Clearing the Environment Daily

Fatigue in an office environment often comes from an excess of positive ions in the environment, created primarily from electronic machinery and lack of oxygen. Aside from the many modern devices available for balancing EMF vibrations to protect office workers, one way you can greatly increase negative ions in your environment is to wash the surface of your desk daily with plain water. Doing so every time you empty your trash can assure you a clean and healthy environment in which to work.

Putting greater attention into relating your office to the bagua and balancing your whole work environment will have a dramatic effect on your creativity and success. Then, sit back and enjoy the ride. Miracles *can* happen!

Chapter 15

Infinite Connections

Feng Shui in the Body

It is possible to see another manifestation of the bagua and the trigrams of the *I Ching* when looking at the human body. As a trained physiognomist knows well, "the face never lies," and it is here that the bagua appears most clearly.

Because we are not separate from our environment, our face and our house are closely related. The Front Door to the face is the mouth; this means that it occupies the Water position. The house of Fire, symbolizing Illumination or Enlightenment, encompasses the area of the pineal gland, also known as the third eye. Each of the remaining houses is now easy to locate, and the bagua takes on new meaning as an expression of our life.

Many other symbols of the eight trigrams can be included when we personalize the bagua by using it to look at our face. For example, darkness around the mouth, indicating stagnation in Water, reveals the beginning of problems on The Journey, our path in life. Blemishes in Thunder or Lake are a sign of clutter that will be present simultaneously in these same areas in our home and our life. To the experienced eye, the face reveals as much about a person's destiny through feng shui as a good floor plan or photograph of the house.

The whole human body is also a reflection of the whole bagua. Problems with any part will appear both in the places where we live and work and in the events of our daily life. A deeper study of traditional Chinese medicine and the trigrams as symbols in the body reveal the inescapable connections we have with our environment.

Differences Between Man and Woman

In one way, gender determines destiny. As a result of who we are biologically, a man will never give birth to a child, nor will a woman manufacture sperm to plant inside another woman's womb. The Universal Opposites of Heaven and Earth, called yang and yin, symbolize the energies of Man and Woman. The trigram for Heaven is composed of three unbroken lines (all yang); the trigram for Earth is made up of three broken lines (all yin).

The shape of our house is like the genetic marker of our personal gender. However we may dress or whatever our sexual orientation, underneath it all is a biological distinction that exists even before birth. We may add lilacs and lace to a house whose shape creates a greater yang charge, but the *structure* still carries a predominant energy.

When either of the primary yang (Heaven) or yin (Earth) houses is missing from the bagua inside your home or workplace, creating negative space, it will be difficult for the gender whose house is absent to feel settled there for a long period. Naturally, this effect will vary among individuals, some men having developed more of their feminine, receptive nature and some women having developed more of their masculine, creative energy.

But these symbols carry other charges beyond simple personality traits. The Destiny Chart that follows expands upon the energies that are present in the bagua as they relate to the trigrams. They can be seen as complementary antagonisms for the following aspects:

Destiny Chart

Yang	*Yin*
Material	Spiritual
The Self	Selflessness
Physical	Emotional
Intellect	Intuition

A house in which there is a projection in Heaven or Earth or in the two trigrams directly opposite this complementary pair, Wind and Mountain, will embody exaggerated energies of yang or yin, respectively. When it appears as if the house shape also carries a charge of negative space, the correlated energies of yin and yang, as listed in the Destiny Chart, will be missing.

Special care should be taken when considering a house or office of an extremely unusual, unbalanced shape. Although the effect of negative space can be reduced, it is nearly impossible to erase it entirely.

In the figure below, the houses of Wind and Heaven are projections, accentuating forces of yang related to these energies. In general, men will be happy in this house, and women will find it uncomfortable. Both male and female occupants are more likely to be focused on materialism, the intellect, and developing the self. Paradoxically, when people who live in houses this shape are successful, they will more naturally become Helpful People, charged with Heaven's energy.

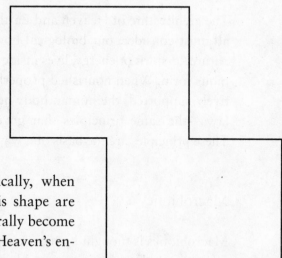

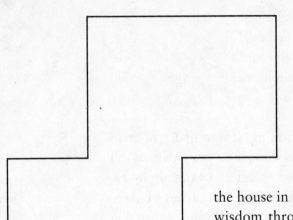

In the following figure, Earth and Mountain can be considered projections, increasing the charge of yin energy. Women will feel more settled here, and most men will feel uncomfortable being here for long periods. This house's occupants are more likely to be aware of their intuition and emotions and to have a spirit of selflessness, not nearly as able to accumulate wealth or material possessions as the occupants of the house in the previous figure. This house creates wisdom through life experience, which will carry more material difficulties but with a greater emotional and spiritual maturity.

Your body is a temple.
THE HOLY BIBLE

The architecture of Heaven and Earth is perfect in the one house we all must consider: our biological home, the human body. Our true nature, as spirit or energy, lives inside a perfectly ordered and harmonious form. When nourished properly, cleared of clutter, and sensitively supported, the human body heals itself as a result of natural laws—the same principles that govern the external environment. These principles are the basis of a way of life known as macrobiotics.

Macrobiotics

Macrobiotics is thought by most people to be a dietary practice that incorporates brown rice, vegetables, and other foods consumed in certain ratios. The majority of those who know little about it believe it to be a diet that is restrictive, bland, and even dangerous, practiced by food extremists without regard to modern science.

Consider the possibility that most of what you think you know about macrobiotics is really just a mishmash. Imagine that you have opened a box containing 237 pieces from thirteen jigsaw puzzles, each needing 100 pieces to complete a whole picture. Most of every puzzle would be unfinished, and you'd more than likely have only a faint idea of what any of them looked like.

Macrobiotics is not a diet at all, but a way of life based on timeless principles of *change* and *choice*. By gradually introducing certain simple foods, exercises, and practices into your everyday life, you begin to bring into focus a harmony and order that is already present. To be aware of this order, you really need not give up anything at all, unless you choose to, but it is clear from years of practice by millions of people throughout the world that consumption of whole, natural foods allows you to have a greater role in guiding your own life.

No foods are forbidden except when your body tells
you so.

LIMA OHSAWA, Macrobiotic Cuisine

Whole cereal grains, like brown rice, corn, oats, wheat, and barley, and whole-grain products, like breads, pancakes, crackers, pastas, and puddings, have been the staple foods of most cultures throughout the centuries.

In ancient Greece the word *macrobiotics* was used for the art of achieving health and longevity through living in harmony with the environment. In modern times, the term was recovered by the Japanese philosopher Georges Ohsawa to represent the healthy way of life, reflecting the spirit of how a healthy person views life: macro, meaning "large or great," and bios, meaning "life." More specifically, with proper diet we can experience a great life, full of adventure, freedom, and creativity. Ohsawa spent the better part of his life spreading macrobiotic philosophy and dietary reform throughout the world. Since his death in the mid-1960s, several of his friends and students—now highly respected teachers—have carried on his work.

The macrobiotic approach is one that takes into account the evolution of humanity, our relation to the environment, and our individual needs. The diet is not only a preventive one, aiming to maintain good health and to decrease the incidence of sickness; it is also used therapeutically by those who are already ill and wish to use natural means of healing.

Although the principles of macrobiotic eating are practices in many traditional cultures, the philosophical basis of macrobiotics is the study of change; namely, the principles of relativity or yin and yang, the basis of all Eastern philosophies, cultures, arts, and medicine.

The Unifying Principle

By observing our day-to-day thoughts and activity, we can easily see that everything is in motion, or in other words, everything changes; electrons spin around a central nucleus in the atom; the earth rotates on its axis while orbiting the sun; the solar system is revolving around the galaxy; and the galaxies are moving away from one another with enormous movement. An orderly *pattern* is discernible, however. Day follows night; winter changes to summer and then back to winter again; during the day we stand up and are active, and at night we lie down and rest.

Starting from this basic understanding, we can classify all phenomena into either one or the other of the two categories: yin and yang. Because these are relative terms, nothing in the world is absolutely yin or absolutely yang, however; all phenomena possess both in varying degrees.

Yin and yang are always changing into each other in a continual cycle, reflected in the change from night to day and winter to summer, from inhaling to exhaling. Contraction, or yang, produces heat, which eventually causes the expansion of yin; expansion produces coldness, which then causes contraction. As a result, vegetation growing in a more yin, or cold, northern climate is usually smaller, while the vegetation in more yang, or hot, climates is usually larger.

Diet and Health

An appreciation of the importance of proper diet for good health has been largely lost in modern times. Among more primitive societies it was well recognized and used as the basis of medicine. Food is our source of being. Through the vegetable kingdom, all the basic forces of life are combined in a form that can be used by the human organism. Sunlight, soil, water, and air are taken in through the medium of the vegetable kingdom. To eat is to take in the whole environment.

The dietary approach of macrobiotics is not to prescribe a specific diet. Because we are all different—live in different environments, have diverse needs, and do different work—individual diets will vary.

Today, hundreds of thousands of people around the world use macrobiotic principles to select and prepare their daily diet and to restore their health and happiness. Hundreds of centers all over the world focus on educating people about macrobiotic principles.

Classification

To develop a balanced diet, it is essential to classify foods into categories of yin and yang. Different factors in the growth and structure of foods can indicate whether a food is predominantly yin or yang. Because all foods have both yin and yang qualities, in classifying foods we must look for the factors that dominate.

Yin Energy Creates	*Yang Energy Creates*
Growth in a hot climate	Growth in a cold climate
Foods containing water	Foods that are dry
Fruits and leaves	Stems, roots, and seeds
Growth high above the ground	Growth below ground
Hot, aromatic foods	Salty, sour foods

One of the most accurate methods of classification is by the cycle of growth in food plants. During the winter, the climate is very cold (yin); during this time of year the growing energy descends into the root system. Leaves wither and die as the sap descends to the roots and the vitality of the plant becomes more condensed. Plants that are used for food and grown in the late autumn and winter are more dry and have a more concentrated quality. They can be kept for a long time without spoiling. Examples are roots such as carrots, parsnips, turnips, and onions.

During the spring and early summer, many plants' energy ascends and new greens appear as the weather becomes more hot (yang). These plants are more yin in nature. Summer vegetables are more watery and perish quickly. They provide a cooling effect that is needed in warm months. In late summer, the growing energy has reached its zenith, and the fruits become ripe. They are generally watery and sweet and develop higher above the ground.

This yearly cycle can be applied to the part of the world in which a food originates. Foods that find their origin in hot tropical climates where the vegetation is lush and abundant are more yin, while foods that come from colder climates are more yang.

We can classify different foods that grow at the same time of year by seeing their general growth pattern. The root system is governed by yang energy, the tendency to descend. The stem and leaves are governed by yin energy. This energy is expressed in the dominant direction of growth.

The Importance of Cereal Grains

For centuries, humanity has looked to cereal grains as the primary food—the pulse of mankind. This is especially true of the great civilizations of the world. The importance of the cereal grains in the evolution of humanity cannot be overlooked. Recently, consumption of whole grains has sharply fallen and has been replaced by animal quality foods, such as dairy foods and meat, and refined carbohydrates, such as sugar and refined flour. It is now widely recognized that this shift in diet has led to the development of many of the major health problems in our technological civilization.

The cereal grains are unique among our foods; they are both the beginning and the end of the vegetal cycle, combining seed and fruit. It is for these reasons as well as the cereals' ability to combine well with other vegetables to provide a wholesome diet that cereals form the most important single food in the macrobiotic regimen.

Preparation

Macrobiotic cooking is unique. The ingredients are simple, and cooking is the key to producing meals that are nutritious, tasty, and attractive. The cook has the ability to change the quality of the food. More cooking—the use of pressure, salt, heat, and time—makes the energy of food more concentrated. Quick cooking and little salt preserves the lighter qualities of the food. A good cook controls the health of those for whom he or she cooks by varying the many different cooking styles.

Chewing is an important complement to the macrobiotic diet. It can also be thought of as a form of preparation. A meal should be eaten calmly and with gratitude. One of the best ways of expressing this gratitude is by chewing well so that the food we eat can be digested well and used by the body more efficiently.

The Macrobiotic Way

Macrobiotics is really a common sense approach to eating. Diet is the single most important factor in the rise of degenerative illness. In light of the incidence of degenerative illness and general poor health that plagues the world, the macrobiotic approach is a sensible alternative to our overprocessed and devitalized foods. The return to a diet more in keeping with that of our ancestors is in order if human-ity is to regain its health and vitality.

Macrobiotics is, very simply, *internal* feng shui. *You can do nothing more powerful to transform your life than to follow a diet and way of life based upon macrobiotic principles.* Balancing the inner bagua through daily food is the real key to the practice of intuitive feng shui. It is *true* freedom.

References

Feng Shui, Geomancy, Architecture, Design, Puzzles, and Patterns

Alexander, Christopher. *A Pattern Language* (New York: Oxford University Press, 1987).

———. *A Timeless Way of Building* (New York: Oxford University Press, 1987).

Chang, Amos Ih Tiao. *Tao of Architecture* (Princeton, NJ: Princeton University Press, 1956).

Davies, Paul. *The Cosmic Blueprint* (New York: Simon & Schuster, 1988).

Eitel, Ernest J. *Feng Shui: The Science of Sacred Landscape in Old China* (London: Synergetic Press, 1984).

Gallagher, Winnifred. *Power of Place: How Our Surroundings Shape Our Thoughts, Emotions & Actions* (New York: Simon & Schuster, 1993).

Groves, Derham. *Feng Shui and Western Building Ceremonies* (Dumfriesshire, Scotland: Tynron Press, 1991).

Lawlor, Robert. *Sacred Geometry: Philosophy and Practice* (New York: Thames and Hudson, 1982).

Lip, Evelyn. *Feng Shui: A Layman's Guide to Chinese Geomancy* (Union City, CA: Heian International, 1987).

Makinson, Randell L. *Greene & Greene, Architecture as a Fine Art* (Salt Lake City, Utah: Peregrine Smith Books, 1977).

Mitchell, John. *The Earth Spirit: Its Ways, Shrines and Mysteries* (New York: Thames and Hudson, 1989).

Morgan, Jim. *The Wonders of Magic Squares* (New York: Vintage, 1982).

O'Brien, Joanne. *The Elements of Feng Shui* (Shaftesbury, Dorset: Element Books Limited Longmead, 1991).

Olivastro, Dominic. *Ancient Puzzles* (New York: Bantam Books, 1993).

Pearson, David. *The Natural House Book* (New York: Simon & Schuster, 1989).

Pennick, Nigel. *The Ancient Science of Geomancy* (New York: Thames and Hudson, 1979).

———. *Earth Harmony* (London: Rider Book/Century Paperback, 1987).

Purce, Jill. *The Mystic Spiral: Journey of the Soul* (New York: Thames and Hudson, 1990).

Rossbach, Sarah. *Feng Shui* (New York: E. P. Dutton, 1983).

———. *Interior Design with Feng Shui* (New York: E. P. Dutton, 1987).

Schimmel, Annemarie. *The Mystery of Numbers* (New York: Oxford, 1993).

Sharp, Dennis. *Illustrated Encyclopedia of Architects and Architecture* (New York: Quarto Publishing, 1991).

Skinner, Stephen. *The Living Earth Manual of Feng Shui* (London: Arkana, 1989).

Swartwout, Glen, M.D. *Electromagnetic Pollution Solutions* (Hilo, Hawaii: Aerai Publishing, 1991).

Walters, Derek. *Feng Shui: The Chinese Art of Designing a Harmonious Environment* (New York: Simon & Schuster, 1988).

I Ching, Astrology, Divination

Anthony, Carol K. *A Guide to the I Ching* (Stowe, MA: Anthony Publishing Company, 1988).

————. *The Philosophy of the I Ching* (Stowe, MA: Anthony Publishing Company, 1981).

Chung-Yuan, Chang. *Creativity and Taoism: A Study of Chinese Philosophy, Art and Poetry* (New York: Harper & Row, 1970).

Cleary, Thomas. *The Essential Confucius* (New York: HarperCollins, 1993).

————. *The Taoist I Ching* (Boston: Shambhala, 1986).

Dukes, Shifu Terence. *Chinese Hand Analysis* (York Beach, ME: Samuel Weiser, 1994).

Hazel, Peter. *Ancient Chinese I Ching: Consulting the Coins* (Selangor Darul Eshan, Malaysia: Pelanduk Publications, 1990).

Hoefler, Angelika. *I Ching: New Systems, Methods & Revelations* (Wilmot, WI, 1988).

Kushi, Michio. *Nine Star Ki: Introducing Oriental Astrology* (Becket, MA: One Peaceful World Press, 1992).

Lau, Theodora. *The Handbook of Chinese Horoscopes* (New York: Harper & Row, 1980).

Lingerman, Hal A. *The Book of Numerology* (York Beach, ME: Samuel Weiser, 1994).

Lorusso, Julia, and Joel Glick. *Strategems: A Mineral Perspective* (Alberquerque, NM: Brotherhood of Life, 1985).

Mann, A. T. *The Round Art* (Cheltenham, Great Britain: Dragon's World, 1979).

Ou-i, Chih-hsu. *The Buddhist I Ching* (Boston: Shambhala, 1987).

Palmer, Martin, Kwok Man Ho, and Joanne O'Brien. *The Fortune Teller's I Ching* (New York: Ballantine Books, 1986).

Palmer, Martin. *T'ung Shu: The Ancient Chinese Almanac* (London: Rider and Company, 1986).

Post, James Nathan. *64 Keys: An Introductory Guide to the I Ching* (Cottonwood, AZ: Cottonwood Press, 1978).

Shchutskii, Iulian K. *Researches on the I Ching* (London: Routledge & Kegan Paul, 1980)

Sherrill, W. A., and W. K. Chu. *An Anthology of I Ching* (London: Arkana, 1989).

———. *Astrology of I Ching* (York, ME: Samuel Weiser, 1976).

Shimano, Jimmei. *Oriental Fortune Telling* (Rutland, VT: Charles E. Tuttle, 1956).

Sorrell, Roderic, and Amy Max Sorrell. *The I Ching Made Easy* (San Francisco: HarperSanFrancisco, 1994).

Blofeld, John, trans. *I Ching (The Book of Change)* (New York: E. P. Dutton, 1968).

Huang, Kerson and Rosemary Huang, trans. *I Ching* (New York: Workman Publishing, 1987).

Waley, Arthur. *Three Ways of Thought in Ancient China* (Stanford, CA: Stanford University Press, 1956).

Whincup, Greg. *Rediscovering the I Ching* (Wellingborough, England: Aquarian Press, 1987).

Wilhelm, Hellmut. *Change: Eight Lectures on the I Ching* (New York: Pantheon Books, 1960).

Wilhelm, R. *I Ching or Book of Changes,* trans. C. F. Baynes (Princeton, NJ: Princeton University Press, 1950).

Wing, R. L. *The Illustrated I Ching* (Wellingborough, England: Aquarian, 1987).

Yoshikawa, Takashi. *The Ki* (New York: St. Martin's Press, 1986).

Yu-Lan, Fung. *A Short History of Chinese Philosophy* (New York: Macmillan Company, 1950).

Macrobiotics and Healing

Aihara, Herman. *Basic Macrobiotics* (Tokyo: Japan Publications, 1985).

Bates, W. H., M.D. *Better Eyesight Without Glasses* (New York: Holt, Rinehart and Winston, 1920)

Colbin, Annmarie. *Food and Healing* (New York: Ballantine Books, 1986).

Dossey, Larry, M.D. *Healing Words: The Power of Prayer and the Practice of Medicine* (San Francisco: HarperSanFrancisco, 1993).

Heidenry, Carolyn. *An Introduction to Macrobiotics* (Wayne, NJ: Avery, 1987).

———. *Making the Transition to a Macrobiotic Diet* (Wayne, NJ: Avery, 1984).

Kushi, Michio. *Book of Do In: Exercises for Physical and Spiritual Development* (Tokyo: Japan Publications, 1979).

———. *The Book of Macrobiotics* (Tokyo: Japan Publications, 1987).

———. *Macrobiotic Way: The Complete Macrobiotic Diet and Exercise Book* (Wayne, NJ: Avery Publishing Group, 1985).

Northrup, Christiane, M.D. *Women's Bodies, Women's Wisdom* (New York: Bantam Books, 1994).

Ohsawa, Georges. *Cancer and the Philosophy of the Far East* (Oroville, CA: Georges Ohsawa Macrobiotic Foundation, 1981).

———. *Philosophy of Oriental Medicine: Key to Your Personal Judging Ability* (Oroville, CA: Georges Ohsawa Macrobiotic Foundation, 1991).

Turner, Kristina. *The Self-Healing Cookbook* (Vashon Island, WA: Earthtones Press, 1989).

Veith, Ilza. *The Yellow Emperor's Classic of Internal Medicine* (Berkeley: University of California Press, 1972).

Inspiration, Consciousness

Boorstin, Daniel J. *The Discoverers* (New York: Random House, 1983).

Capra, Fritjof. *The Tao of Physics* (Boulder, CO: Shambhala, 1975).

Castaneda, Carlos. *The Art of Dreaming* (New York: Harper Collins, 1993).

————. *A Separate Reality* (New York: Simon & Schuster, 1972).

du Noüy, Lecomte. *Human Destiny* (New York: Longmans, Green, 1947).

Hayward, Jeremy W. *Perceiving Ordinary Magic* (Boston: Shambhala, 1984).

Jahn, Robert G., and Brenda J. Dunne. *Margins of Reality: The Role of Consciousness in the Physical World* (San Diego, CA: Harcourt, Brace, Jovanovich, 1987).

Moyne, John and Coleman Barks. *Open Secret: Versions of Rumi* (Putney, VT: Threshold Books, 1984).

Rinpoche, Sogyal. *The Tibetan Book of Living and Dying* (San Francisco: HarperSanFrancisco, 1992).

Rumi, Jeláluddin. *Like This* (Athens, GA: Maypop, 1990).

————. *The Ruins of the Heart* (Putney, VT: Threshold Books, 1981).

Sagan, Carl. *The Dragons of Eden* (New York: Ballantine, 1977).

Senge, Peter M. *The Fifth Discipline* (New York: Doubleday, 1990).

Trungpa, Chögyam. *The Sacred Path of the Warrior* (Boston: Shambhala, 1988).

Tsu, Lao. *Tao Te Ching* (New York: Vintage Books, 1972).

Index

Heaven (Helpful Friends): in bagua of home, 101–2; symbolism of, 57; trigram of, 56; visualization for, 43, 49
Heaven's force, 32–33
Heavy objects, 144–45
Heschel, Rabbi Abraham, 97
Hotel case history, 152–53
House plans: bagua aligned with, 77–80; fixed placements in, 84; fluid placements in, 84–86; mirrors to define space of, 126; showing negative space, 80–81; showing projections, 82–83
Houses: arriving at, 65–67; bagua of, 4, 12, 55–60, 77–80, 91–107; bedrooms/sleeping areas of, 88–89; clearing spaces in, 153–56; first impressions of, 62–63; the Front Door of, 70; kitchens in, 87–88; living areas of, 89–90; odd-shaped, 73; Predecessor Law and, 150–51; selecting artwork for, 143–44; symmetrical shaped, 72
Hugo, Victor, 69
Human Destiny (Du Noüy), 31

I Ching (*Book of Changes*): author's introduction to, 2–5; feng shui and, 27; Lo Map of the, 60; space arrangement detailed in, 29; working knowledge of, 53–55
Impulsive Opposites, 55–56
Inner Knowledge, 104
Inner voice, 68
Internal clarity, 117
Intuition, 116–17
Intuitive feng shui, 29–30, 75

Ki (life force), 27. *See also* Energy
King Wen, 54, 69
Kissinger, Henry, 4

Kitchens: stove placement in, 87–88; using mirrors in, 124
Koran, 134
Kuan's Geomantic Indicator, 5
Kübler-Ross, Elisabeth, 97
Kushi, Michio, 5

Lady S. case history, 128, 130
Lake (Creativity): of bagua in home, 103; visualization for, 50
Landmarks, 31–32
Lao Tsu, 13, 25, 80, 93, 169
Lights, 134–35
Lin, Yun, 5–6
"Little Mountain House, The," 112–13
Living areas, 89–90
Living spaces, 11
Lo Map, 54, 60
Lo Map Later Heaven sequence, 55
Longbarrows, 33
Lucy's case history, 109–10
Luo pan, 4, 26

Macrobiotics, 190–92, 195–96; as internal feng shui, 196. *See also* Food
Madam H. case history, 139–40
Magic square, 1–3, 54–55, 70–73
Malleable baguas, 70–71
Mallet, Dave, 173
Masculine principle, 101
Metal, 166
Mirrors: convex, 124–25; as a cure, 123–28; described, 119–20; functions of, 120–23
Mountain (Contemplation): of bagua in home, 104–5; symbolism of, 57; trigram of, 56; visualization for, 51
Music, 138
Mysterious Principles of the Universe, 5

About the Author

William Spear is an internationally recognized educator, consultant, lecturer and writer on feng shui, the *I Ching,* geomancy, oriental philosophy, and macrobiotic medicine. He travels extensively worldwide, leading seminars and workshops on a variety of health care issues, including feng shui, natural architecture, vital design, health issues, and the environmental causes of degenerative disease.

In 1984, he founded an educational association for the study and treatment of environmentally related disease, and he continues to serve as its executive director. In addition to numerous television and radio program appearances, Mr. Spear has spoken at the United Nations on environmental issues and consulted in the urban planning process for many community organizations and corporate leaders.

He was the first honorary president of the International Feng Shui Society headquartered in the United Kingdom, where he offers his introductory seminar, "The Transforming Power of Intuitive Feng Shui."

As well as offering many introductory and advanced courses to the general public, he conducts a professional training program in intuitive feng shui for architects, designers, and practitioners and maintains a private practice in New York, London, and Litchfield, Connecticut. To contact the author for additional information in the United States, please write or telephone:

William Spear
24 Village Green Drive
Litchfield, Connecticut 06759
tel: (860) 567-8801
fax: (860) 567-3304

To contact the author in the United Kingdom or for additional information on the professional training program and private consultation services, write or telephone:

Feng Shui Network International
P.O. Box 2133
London W1A 1RL, United Kingdom
tel: (0171) 935-8935
fax: (0171) 935-9295

For inquiries through the Internet, contact the following e-mail address:
fengshuime@aol.com